MW00576189

PRAISE FOR *IMMUTABLE*

JJ is right. Product managers work in complex, dynamic systems. *IMMUTABLE* takes us back to the fundamentals, which is often what we need to do to thrive in chaos. It's a great book to add to your product management book collection. Make use of it when you need practical advice and guidance. JJ is right there with you.

—Adrienne Tan

Co-Founder and Chief Executive Officer, Brainmates

A guide for hiring managers on the product management role.

—R. Dutt

Author, Radical Product Thinking:
The New Mindset for Innovating Smarter

I have mentored and managed product managers for many years. This book successfully captures the key traits that all product managers need, and more importantly, provides simple tools to help them along the journey. JJ's thoughtful recommendations are relevant and practical, making this book a useful guide for both new and experienced product managers.

—Gyanda Sachdeva

Vice President of Product, LinkedIn

JJ is spot on with these truths. Not only has she captured the essence of product management, but she's done so in such a thoughtful way. No matter where you are in your product management career journey, these serve as a guiding light in any industry or application.

—Amber Hall

Global Product Strategy Leader, Kohler

IMMUTABLE: 5 Truths of Great Product Managers is a must-read for all emerging and experienced product managers who aspire to deliver meaningful products while authentically leading teams. The author has provided practical roadmaps and toolkits for building product careers from the inside out.

—**Mamuna Oladipo**
Vice President of Product, Shopify

We tend to overcomplicate things in product management. While we do often work with complex issues, I love how JJ has brought us back to the foundation of great product management in *IMMUTABLE*. Every product manager should strive to perfect these 5 truths.

—**Sophia Perl**
Product Lead, DoorDash

As JJ says right up front in the introduction, she's not trying to reinvent the wheel, but rather provide practical advice and tools for effectively navigating the expanding and demanding product manager role. Yes! The world doesn't need another academic tome on how to prioritize your roadmap. It's often the essential soft skills, enumerated in JJ's 5 truths, that separate the exceptional from the merely competent. I learned this early on as a product manager, then again when building strong teams as a product leader. JJ lays out her playbook with the table of contents, then delivers the goods in each chapter. So don't just read this book—put it into practice—and if you're a product leader, give this gift to your team.

—**David Nash**
Chief Product Officer, Board International,
and Product Management Executive Mentor

I have worked in product management for over ten years, and there is always a trend or a new system, but however you slice it, there are some basic truths. This book is a simple and practical consolidation of the critical skills needed to be an analytical and successful product manager. No matter where you are in your product career, this is a gem of a book to reference.

—Farah Rana
Product Leader, Riot Games

The simplicity of this approach is its power. JJ guides the reader through these critical skills in a down-to-earth manner with real examples and practical advice that anyone can implement. It's an easy and fun read, and there is something for everyone in *IMMUTABLE*.

—Bruce Busby
Product Manager, Intralox

We often think about the success criteria of our products, but what about measuring our success as product managers? JJ's *IMMUTABLE* helps you define the metrics that differentiate good and great PMs, leaving you with actionable insights to succeed. A must read for new and experienced product managers alike looking to accelerate their career growth.

—Nancy Wang
Product Manager, Microsoft

There are two ways product managers can look at their job, outside-in, where you focus on the customer and their problem and you work backward, or you look inside-out, where you figure out who you are, your personal traits and previous experiences to solve a problem. Regardless of which approach your organization works in, or you personally prefer, you still need to deliver value. JJ is right, these five skills make the biggest difference and make you immutable.

Whether you are an associate product manager or a CPO, these skills will help you deliver some incredible value to your customers. However, these five skills are not just for product managers; they are life skills that you can put to use tomorrow in whatever project you are working on. You will be immutable by the incredible stories and advice from others in the field, presented by JJ Rorie, a master communicator.

—Baraa Safaa Ali
Product Leader, Amazon

In *IMMUTABLE*, JJ gives you straightforward, practical advice on the core skills every product manager needs. All I ask, after reading these secrets of great product management, is that you use your talents wisely and only build products that make our world a better place, for everyone! Enjoy!

—Kirsten Zverina Archer
Founder/Product Manager, Abethos Ventures

This is an easy and great read full of practical advice and real examples. This book is applicable to all product managers, regardless of industry, type of product, or experience level. There is something for everyone in *IMMUTABLE*. The power of this book: JJ writes about these *IMMUTABLE* Truths because she's lived them!

—Andy Bowden
Head of Product, Buurst

This book is a roadmap for being a high-performing product manager and a highly sought-after professional. The approachable yet straight-forward style makes it easy to follow. While the exercises she encourages us to practice aren't easy, she is very persuasive in explaining why they are the right questions to pursue.

—Emi Ashida
Product Manager, Kaiser Permanente

In *IMMUTABLE*, JJ Rorie has captured the bedrock characteristics that lead to product management success. It's filled with stories to illustrate the 5 truths, based on her years of experience leading and consulting with product teams. And good news! While these characteristics are fundamental, you can continuously improve in every area, which is exactly why you need this book. JJ provides specific actions you can take to strengthen your abilities.

I recommend the book to anyone seeking to have a bigger impact in product management.

—Nils Davis
Author, The Secret Product Manager Handbook

IMMUTABLE

IMMUTABLE

5 Truths of
Great
Product Managers

JJ RORIE

For permission requests, write to the publisher, addressed "Attention: Permissions Coordinator," at the address below.

Publish Your Purpose
141 Weston Street, #155
Hartford, CT, 06141

The opinions expressed by the Author are not necessarily those held by Publish Your Purpose.

Ordering Information: Quantity sales and special discounts are available on quantity purchases by corporations, associations, and others. For details, contact the publisher at orders@publishyourpurposepress.com.

Edited by: Nancy Graham-Tillman
Proofread by: Chloë Siennah
Cover design by: Cornelia Murariu
Typeset by: Medlar Publishing Solutions Pvt Ltd., India

Printed in the United States of America.
ISBN: 978-1-955985-53-6 (hardcover)
ISBN: 978-1-955985-52-9 (paperback)
ISBN: 978-1-955985-54-3 (ebook)

Library of Congress Control Number: 2022909811

First edition, June 2022.

Publish Your Purpose is a hybrid publisher of non-fiction books. Our authors are thought leaders, experts in their fields, and visionaries paving the way to social change—from food security to anti-racism. We give underrepresented voices power and a stage to share their stories, speak their truth, and impact their communities. Do you have a book idea you would like us to consider publishing? Please visit PublishYourPurpose.com for more information.

DEDICATION

To Mark and Paula,

*Thanks to you, I have always believed
I could do anything, even this.*

Mark, I so wish you were here to see it.

To Gail,

You make me better. Life with you makes perfect sense.

CONTENTS

Truth #1
Great Product Managers have Exceptionally
High Customer Intelligence   1

Truth #2
Great Product Managers are Experts
at Building Relationships   33

Truth #3
Great Product Managers are Master Communicators   57

Truth #4
Great Product Managers have Uncommonly
Good Judgment   73

Truth #5
Great Product Managers are Fanatical About
Prioritizing Their Time   105

INTRODUCTION

When I started thinking about writing a book, my original intent was to generally (and magically?) help people be successful in product management careers by teaching them a specific, great way to do it. But there is no one, specific way. There are lots of ways that can work. Each product manager has a different experience than the next. Of course, there are some similarities. Hang out with the product management community on Twitter (I highly recommend #prodmgmt) or in one of the awesome product management communities around the world, and you will see and hear some common themes surrounding why product management is the most glorious, ridiculous, fun, difficult, stupid, and rewarding profession around. You will also hear how everyone's environment is a bit different and receive lots of "it depends" responses to questions about how something should work.

Product management is not a rigid, fully automated type of endeavor. It is nuanced. It looks, acts, and behaves differently in every organization. Anyone who tells you there is only one way to "do" product management is wrong. Product management is a system of interconnected activities, people, data, incentives, objectives, predictions, and decisions. With all that nuance and all those conditions, there is no way that it can be the same across various companies. I have worked with hundreds of organizations, and each of them has a slightly different product management function.

So, I started doing some soul searching. As with developing a product, a process in which we like to build once for many, I wanted to find the elements that really are consistent across all great product managers regardless of the industry, type of product, or company environment.

Through my research and work, I kept seeing some underlying conditions that are common among all successful product managers. This book is about those conditions—those immutable truths that anchor product managers in skills that lead to success and are truly transferable from one company to another. While product management at the next company may look slightly different from the former one, these skills—the immutable truths—are the foundation on which to continually build success in any environment.

If you read this book and find the suggestions too complicated to implement, frankly I have failed. Though product management is complex, the underlying skills that help us navigate that complexity are not. It takes work and persistence, but these are skills that anyone can become adept in. I truly believe that. That is the entire reason for this book: to help every product manager in the world build an underlying set of immutable skills. The need for these skills will never change. Product management will change around us, but these skills and abilities will always anchor us.

As you read this book, you may find that the concepts within are not that groundbreaking. I am certainly not the first person to say product managers need to understand their customers or communicate ideas effectively. Again, that is the point. I am not trying to reinvent the wheel here; I am trying to give real, practical advice and tools for building a foundation that will help you better navigate the demands of the role. If you have this foundation, no matter where you go in your product management career from here on out, you will be successful.

I hope you enjoy the book and find some valuable nuggets to take with you on your product management journey.

THE GREAT PRODUCT MANAGER AND THEIR IMMUTABLE TRUTHS

A product manager defines the long-term vision of a product by keenly understanding customer needs, market dynamics, and company goals and then collaborates with a cross-functional team to execute that vision. It is a role that requires a balance of often contrary skills and behaviors. Product managers must be both visionaries and tacticians, data analysts and storytellers, leaders and doers. They must be motivated by individual ambitions while also being a collaborative teammate.

Before we go much further, I want to define "greatness" in the context of the product manager role. First, I do not think greatness is a ridiculous goal that can only be achieved by a select few. I also do not believe it should take a grueling 60+ hours a week to achieve greatness as a product manager. If striving to be great ends up taking a toll on your physical and mental health, then we need to redefine greatness. I believe being great as a product manager should have a positive impact on both your professional life and your personal life. The work of great product managers energizes their lives, and their lives motivate and strengthen their work. They put the time into work as needed but also allow themselves to step away and rejuvenate. That is success. That is greatness.

Many organizations grade a product manager by looking at their product's results, mainly via product sales or usage. That will likely be one way we are always assessed as product managers. After all, we are at least partly responsible for the business impacts of our products. But I believe this is a largely ineffective way to measure greatness in a product manager. On one hand, there are so many variables that lead to a product's success or lack thereof. Yes, the product manager should help orchestrate the moving parts of those variables, but they do not control them all. I have seen excellent product managers work on unsuccessful products. The organizational cards were stacked against them, and it was too much to overcome. On the other hand, I have also seen mediocre product managers work on hugely successful products. They inherited a great product or are surrounded by an overachieving team that makes up for their shortcomings.

Another way I see organizations measure the success of product managers is through output, or how many products or features they release. This is a terrible gauge of greatness. Product is the quintessential example of "quality over quantity." I would much prefer one release that truly adds value for the customer than ten releases that are all fluff. I am still surprised at the number of organizations that have an implicit system of currency exchange: funding or prioritization is the loan that must be paid back in the form of output from the product team.

And of course, there are also skills-based assessments that can grade a product manager. Some of these are valuable from a key performance indicator perspective. A high level of capability can be indicative of future performance, but I think this evaluates the means, not the end.

I like to assess greatness in a product manager by looking for the following markers. These markers may not be as quantifiable as product revenue or a self-assessed skills score, but I have found that the folks who embody these have something in common: they anchor themselves in five core capabilities that help them navigate the chaotic world of product management.

- They realize the importance of their role and embrace the challenge that is product management.
- They feel comfortable (most of the time) with their workload and do not constantly feel overwhelmed by the job.
- They are not known as "workaholics." No one doubts their work ethic, but when they do feel overwhelmed, they take time off to rejuvenate. They are also transparent about when they need that time off.

- They enjoy collaborating with teammates. The creative exchange of ideas invigorates them, and they insist on diverse perspectives.
- They change their minds when presented with new, persuasive information or viewpoints.
- They are seen as subject matter experts on more than just "product matters." People ask for their opinions on a wide range of topics.
- They do not leave important things to chance. They are intentional about learning, connecting, and communicating.
- They always seem to have a north star. They rarely appear to be flailing along without a clear direction.

The five core capabilities that allow great product managers to exemplify the above are the five immutable truths on which this book is based. Let me be clear: product managers need more than just these five skills, but these five are the bedrocks to success. The product management world will always be looking for the next great thing that will make us better; this evolution helps us grow and learn. But these immutable truths remain steadfast regardless of the latest fads in frameworks, schools of thought, and methodologies. In my humble opinion, this will always be the foundation needed to consistently succeed in the product manager role.

The five immutable truths of great product managers are:

1) They have exceptionally high customer intelligence.
2) They are experts at building relationships.
3) They are master communicators.
4) They have uncommonly good judgment.
5) They are fanatical about prioritizing their time.

GREAT PRODUCT MANAGERS HAVE EXCEPTIONALLY HIGH CUSTOMER INTELLIGENCE

Rashad, a product manager for a financial services provider, was about six months into his role when, in a meeting with his boss and other leaders, the business unit vice president asked him, "Why do customers buy from us?"

Rashad froze. "Well, we have a great brand. I think customers buy from us because we are well-known and credible."

"Lots of our competitors are well-known. Why don't they buy from them? What makes them choose our product over theirs?" the vice president countered.

Rashad, having spent the past few years as an engineer with the company, began rattling off details about the technology and product features. His comfort zone was in the minutiae, so he naturally reverted to those when put on the spot. After another cringeworthy minute or two, Rashad's boss, Fatima, jumped in.

"The current regulatory environment is causing consternation and a lot more work for financial advisors, and our product provides a streamlined reporting tool that saves them about an hour per week on the mandated reporting requirements. Our competitors still have a bit of a cumbersome reporting function," Fatima succinctly summarized. Satisfied with that retort, the vice president moved on to other discussions.

As Rashad walked out of the meeting, he turned to Fatima and said, "Well, should I start packing my stuff? I blew that."

"No, of course not. You're new in this role. You'll learn. Remember, in product management, our job is to be the expert on the customer problem, not necessarily the expert on the solution," Fatima coached.

Like Rashad, many product managers who are new to the job believe their first responsibility is learning everything there is to know about the product solution. But they first need to learn everything about the customer and the customer's problems. Without this context, the solution may not even meet the needs of the customer. Imagine all the effort that goes into building a product. If we are not even solving the right need in the first place, what is the point?

CUSTOMER INTELLIGENCE

Great product managers have a high level of customer intelligence. This means they have a profound interest in learning about customers and a deep appreciation of important factors that drive customers' behaviors and actions. Ultimately, customer intelligence is used to craft the product's long-term vision. Successful product managers are fierce stewards of the product vision, because they confidently appreciate what is driving customers today and what their likely needs will be in the future.

Here are the four elements of customer intelligence:

1. Customer **characteristics**
2. The **situations and market conditions** customers find themselves in
3. Customer **motivations and drivers**
4. Customer **pain points and unmet needs**

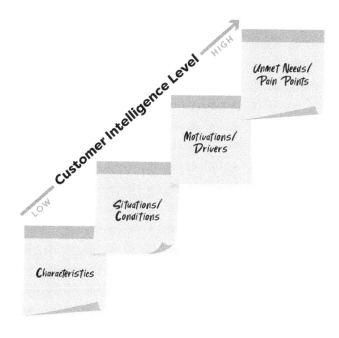

These elements build upon each other, each layer adding to the previous. For example, knowing the general characteristics of a business customer helps us to grasp how market conditions may impact them. Understanding market conditions underlies our ability to uncover their strategic drivers and the pain points that are not being met.

Frankly, most product managers have low- to medium-level customer intelligence because they stop learning at the customer characteristics and market conditions levels. It is the unique job of a product manager to couple that foundational knowledge with a deep comprehension of customers' strategies, goals, stressors, aspirations, and problems. Great product managers perfect the skills it takes to go a layer or two deeper into the customer psyche.

Customer Characteristics

Customer characteristics are the basic traits of the customer. For business customers, they include size, geographic footprint, ownership, and organizational structure. For individual consumers, they include age, gender, household income, and location. Knowing such traits will help lay the groundwork for gaining deeper insights.

If the customer is a business, answer the following questions:

- What is the size of the company? Number of employees? Annual revenue?
- What is the history of the company? When was it founded? What is the story of the founders? Has the company grown organically or through mergers and acquisitions?
- Where is the company located? Where is its headquarters? Where else does the company do business?

- What is the structure of the organization? Are there various business units? Do the units work autonomously or in a more connected way?
- What is the leadership hierarchy? How are teams organized? How are decisions made?
- What is the company's organizational culture? Is it rigid or more flexible in its operations, environment, and expectations? Is the culture formal or more laid back? Is it stringently results-oriented, or does it also have a purpose-driven approach?
- What is the company's approach to work? Does it have an in-person culture, or do many of its employees work remotely?
- What is the company's ownership form? Public? Private? Who owns it?

If your customers are individual consumers, answer these questions instead:

- What are the demographics of the consumer? What is their average age? Race? Gender?
- Where do they live geographically? Do they live in a rural or urban area? Does this have any impact on their access to and use of your product?
- What is their family / household situation? Are they married / partnered? Do they have children?
- What is their household income / financial situation?
- What is their educational background?
- What is their profession?

As you document this information, consider whether any of these characteristics have an impact on access to or use of your product. For example, public companies are often keenly focused on quarterly results and prioritize activities that impact their next quarter or two. Companies owned by private equity firms are often focused on activities that set them up for the best exit. People who live in urban areas often have access to more goods, services, and resources than those who live in some rural areas. Knowing this leads to a better understanding of what's going on with your customers.

Situations and Market Conditions

Your customers participate in communities, do business in particular industries, and live and work in certain geographic regions, all of which undergo changing situations and conditions that impact your customers. These factors can include evolving regulations, economic fluctuations, supply chain disruptions, employment opportunity growth or contraction, and more. Keeping tabs on the matters happening in your customers' surroundings helps lay the groundwork for ultimately understanding motivations and pain points.

For business customers, consider the following questions:

- What trends are permeating the industries in which the company does business?
- What is the regulatory backdrop? Is it a highly regulated industry? To what specific regulations must they adhere?
- What is the competitive landscape? Is it a centralized market with only a few big players, or is it decentralized with many competitors?
- Where is the market in its life cycle? Is it a growing market or is it mature or even declining?

- What is the overall situation for employment? Are companies in the industry generally able to find good talent, or is attracting and retaining a workforce an issue? Are the occupations in the market growing or declining?

For individual consumers, consider these questions:

- What are the economic conditions where your target consumers live?
- Are job prospects high or minimal?
- What are the general costs of living?
- What are the cultural drivers of the area?
- Is there a high or low perception of economic stability?
- Are the markets urban or rural?

Motivations and Drivers

Customers are motivated and driven by many factors, including money, achievement, recognition, stability, health, career growth, fear, and flexibility. To satisfy customer needs and pain points, product managers must first understand the underlying, powerful drivers of their beliefs and behaviors.

For business customers, think about the following:

- What problem is the company trying to solve for its customers?
- What are the company's strategic pillars?
- What are its financial goals?
- Is the company risk-averse, or is it willing to take chances to win big?

- Are employees encouraged and recognized for thinking creatively, or is it uncomfortable when the status quo is challenged?

For individual consumers, think about these questions:

- What is most important to them? Family? Financial success? Health?
- What are their dreams? Do they have specific goals for their future?
- Are they more practical in their buying habits, or do they tend to make impulse purchases?
- Are they interested in social status?
- What are their values? What principles do they live by? Are they altruistic and community-oriented? Do they prefer to prioritize their time with their circle of friends and family?

Pain Points and Unmet Needs

The crescendo of customer intelligence is identifying customers' pain points and unmet needs. The entire point of building the other layers of intelligence is to better understand customers so we can ultimately identify problems to solve for them.

For business customers, answer these questions:

- What keeps members of the company up at night worrying about their jobs?
- What are the barriers that could keep the company from reaching its strategic goals?
- What are the things that are causing the company stress?

- Which business opportunities is the company most excited about?
- If the company could wave a magic wand and change one thing in its business, what would that thing be?

For individual consumers, answer the following:

- What are the things that are stressing them?
- What are they most passionate about?
- If other obligations were not an issue, what would they spend the most time doing?
- What struggles are they having in their lives?
- If they could wave a magic wand and change one thing in their lives, what would that thing be?

THE CUSTOMER CHAIN

"Who is your customer?" I once asked a product manager at a global consumer electronics company.

"Truck drivers. Our product is a dash camera that takes a continuous video of the road around them as they are driving," the product manager answered.

"Okay, so you sell directly to the consumer—the truck driver who uses the product?"

"In some cases, but mostly we sell through retailers. The truck driver buys it at the retail store."

"So, retailers are also a customer?"

"Yes, I suppose so."

"Do you sell directly to the retailers or go through a third party to get your products on their shelves?"

"For some of our products, we sell through distributors. They have the relationships with the retailers to get our products in."

"So, distributors are also a customer?"

"We don't call them customers, but we are always working with the distributor to make sure our products are front and center in their discussions with retailers."

"So, the reality is you have three constituents in your customer chain: distributors, retailers, and the end-user consumer."

"I never thought about it that way, but yes, that makes sense. We do need to be aware of the needs of each of those parties."

Before you can build customer intelligence by identifying the characteristics, situations, motivations, and unmet needs of your customers, you must first firmly understand who all your customers are. A **customer chain** is a representation of the various constituents involved in getting the product from your organization all the way to the end user. The description of the three primary business models used by organizations— business-to-business (B2B), business-to-consumer (B2C), and business-to-government (B2G)—imply a direct and simple relationship, with the latter "B," "C," or "G" representing the one and only customer. However, the simplicity of such models is often not the case. If you sell your product directly to the person or business that uses it, then your chain is simple. But the reality is often more complex for many organizations that sell to a business, which in turn sells to another business or to a consumer who ultimately uses the product. For instance, the consumer electronics company just mentioned uses third party distributors, who then place products with retailers, who then sell to the end-consumer.

So, their customer chain is actually B2B2B2C! Not so simple, especially considering the company must build customer intelligence on each of those constituents. While priority may be given to the end-consumer's needs, there must also be an understanding of the retailer's buying and traffic strategies and what drives the distributor's actions and priorities.

CUSTOMER CHAIN TEMPLATE

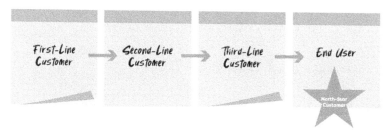

Writing down who your customers are may seem like an elementary exercise, and I suppose it is on some level, but it is also an important one. As my conversation above shows, the more complex the chain, the easier it is to leave a constituent out of consideration. Building intelligence on each customer type and having them all in one place allows you to plan and prioritize which information you need.

First-Line Customers

Your first-line customers are those who directly buy your products from your organization. They typically either resell them in whole to others, combine them with other components or products to create a solution, or otherwise engage in an activity that contributes to your product getting into end-users' hands.

Second-Line Customers

Occasionally, there is a layer between the first-line customer and the end-user. This may be a retailer, a broker, or an original equipment manufacturer (OEM). For example, many automotive parts manufacturers sell their products to components specialists who then transform the parts and raw materials into particular specifications for an OEM such as Volkswagen or Ford. In this case, the auto parts company's second-line customer is the OEM.

Third-Line Customers

In some cases, you may even have a third-line customer before the end-user. For instance, the healthcare industry in the United States is a complex environment with many stakeholders and constituents. (The United States is not the only country with a complex healthcare system, but many other developed nations have a more centralized approach.) The constituents include purchasers such as government or employers; fiscal intermediaries such as insurance companies and group purchasing organizations (those entities that consolidate purchasing power and buy in bulk for many providers); the providers of healthcare such as doctors and nurses; and, ultimately, the patient.

A medical device company may have to work with several of these entities to ultimately have their product used on the patient. In this complex environment, companies often even have a fourth- or fifth-line customer.

End-Users

These are the people who use or directly benefit from your product.

North-Star Customers

The most important part of the customer chain exercise is to identify the north-star customer: the customer whose needs and problems drive product strategy and prioritization and take precedence over other constituents.

Let's look at a few examples of the customer chain, from simple to complex:

Example 1: Software-as-a-Service Podcast Recording Application

This company provides an online application for recording and editing podcast episodes. It sells directly to the end-user through transactions on its website.

First-Line Customer

There is no first-line customer for this company because the end-user is the direct customer.

Second-Line Customer

There is no second-line customer for this company.

Third-Line Customer

There is no third-line customer for this company.

End-User

The end-user is the person who purchases and uses the podcast software.

North-Star Customer

This is simple. There is only one customer in the chain, so of course, the north-star customer is the end-user, the podcaster. The company will focus on keenly understanding and meeting this target customer's needs.

SAAS PODCAST SOFTWARE COMPANY'S CUSTOMER CHAIN

Example 2: Consumer Electronics Company

This company makes cameras that are installed on the dash of vehicles to take continuous recordings of the road. The company targets professional truck drivers and positions its products to that niche group.

First-Line Customer

The first-line customers are the distributors who have long-standing relationships with specialty retailers, specifically truck stops and gas stations. These retailers are important because they are frequented by truck drivers who are the end-users of the company's products.

Second-Line Customer

The second-line customer is the specialty retailer, such as truck stops and gas stations.

Third-Line Customer

There is no third-line customer for this company.

End-User

The end-user is the truck driver who installs the dash camera in their truck to record the road as they drive.

North-Star Customer

This company's north-star customer is the end-user, the truck driver. They are the ones who will use (or not use) the product based on how well it meets their needs. While the distributor and retailer control the ability to get the product in front of the end-user, the retailer will not want it on their shelves if the consumer is not demanding it in the first place.

CONSUMER ELECTRONICS COMPANY'S CUSTOMER CHAIN

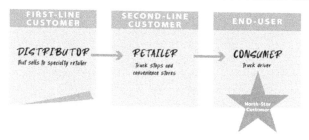

Example 3: Commercial Lighting Company

This company makes commercial lighting for parks and other communal, public spaces. They work with municipalities and local governments and with the bid managers, contractors, and project management firms that run public works projects. Their customer chain is quite complex.

First-Line Customer

The company's first-line customer is typically the general contractor bidding to be the overall manager of the public works project, such as the creation of a new public park. The general contractor is responsible for bringing together all the subcontractors who will be needed for the project, including lighting engineers, landscape architects, and civil planners. The commercial lighting company solicits the general contractor to be the lighting subcontractor for the project.

Second-Line Customer

The company's second-line customer is typically the city bid manager, the person who is responsible for sourcing all services and products necessary for completing the project. They typically put out a public proposal request for the various needs of a project and either select one general contractor to manage all aspects or, if a general contractor does not meet all needs, contract with multiple providers.

If the commercial lighting company is not already subcontracted through a general contractor, they will interact directly with the bid manager.

Third-Line Customer

The third-line customer in this example is the civil planner, the person who is responsible for creating the full plan for the new public park. The plan includes landscape design; lighting; the need for types of play, rest, or other areas; the requirements for sustainability and environmentalism; and all other long-term considerations for the park.

It is important for the commercial lighting company to have a relationship with the civil planner. That way, the company can influence design principals and the engineering of the lighting plan from the beginning of the design process.

Fourth-Line Customer

In this case, there are fourth-line customers working on the project, such as the lighting engineer and the landscape architect. These constituents will work with the civil planner during the design process to determine where lighting is needed and evaluate the requirements regarding glare reduction, light pollution, energy usage, and maintenance costs.

The commercial lighting company would like to have relationships with these constituents so the company can tout its technologies as customizable solutions and understand any need for new innovations.

End-User

The end-user is the individual citizen utilizing the light exuded by the company's product.

North-Star Customer

This is a good example of how the north-star customer is not always the end-user. The citizen using the park would technically be the "user" of the light. The citizen simply wants a well-lit environment for sight and safety. However, the civil planner drives the overall vision of the park, the lighting engineer and landscape architect help design how to make that vision a reality, and the bid manager determines which contractor to use to ultimately implement the project's vision.

The north-star customer is not as apparent in this case. If the commercial lighting company has a good reputation and relationship with the civil planner, the company's sustainable, low-maintenance lighting products can often be incorporated into the park's design from the beginning. Additionally, each time a company is part of a project, whether it wins the bid or not, its leaders learn something new about current urban planning trends that make their way back into the product strategy for future innovations.

The north-star customer in this example is the civil planner.

COMMERCIAL LIGHTING COMPANY'S CUSTOMER CHAIN

You may find that your customer chain is very simple like the podcast software company, very complex like the commercial lighting company, or somewhere in the middle. Regardless, you need to ensure that the product team has a congruent view of the constituents in the chain and have pinpointed the north-star customer. The more complex your situation, the better it is to get the cross-functional team together to complete the chain as a group. This not only ensures that all perspectives are considered but also helps align everyone on priorities.

BUILDING CUSTOMER INTELLIGENCE: STUDY–DISCUSS–OBSERVE

Once you have a clear picture of all the constituents in your customer chain, you can better build a high level of intelligence on each of them. Customer intelligence is not a point-in-time activity. It is naturally underpinned by continuous investigation of the world surrounding our customers. It is a byproduct of persistent curiosity.

There is no shortage of frameworks, methodologies, and expert advice on how to best gather feedback from and intelligence on our customers and markets. Some of them are great; others are mostly fluff. Throughout my years in product management, I have found that it really all comes down to doing three things consistently: studying the world around us, discussing what is happening, and observing our customers' environments with our own eyes. That is it. Study. Discuss. Observe. Those practices, if done consistently, provide everything we need to build a high customer intelligence level. Of course, there are mechanisms within each of these methods that work better than others, and I will discuss some of them below. Remember though, it is about finding a routine that you can commit to and be consistent with. Your world is different from another person reading this book. Make these mechanisms work for you in your environment, and you will be more successful at finding consistency.

The Study–Discuss–Observe method is obviously not rocket science, and frankly, that is one of the main reasons it works. It does not take rocket science to build a high level of customer intelligence; it takes consistency and commitment.

Study

There are a myriad of resources that can build our knowledge on industries, customers, and global happenings. Great product managers are voracious consumers of information from business media, books, podcasts, webinars, conferences, financial reports of customers and competitors, and many other sources that build their knowledge base.

After Rashad's fateful meeting with the vice president of his company, he developed a habit of spending about half an hour each morning reading e-newsletters, watching business news, or otherwise taking in information to learn more about his industry.

He also began reviewing internal customer service logs monthly to identify patterns of customer issues and reading the annual reports of his customers who were public companies. He did all of this simply by making time for studying the world around him, which gave him more knowledge and more confidence.

Great product managers find the time and do not leave information-gathering to chance. Find a habit that works for you. Perhaps mornings do not work, but a midday walk listening to your favorite podcasts fits in well. Any method that allows you to consistently keep in touch with important news and happenings in your relevant industries and environments will work.

Here are some useful methods for studying the world around you:

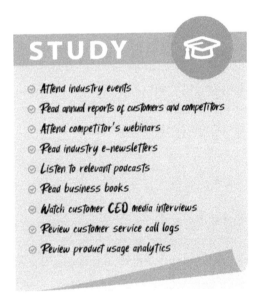

STUDY

- Attend industry events
- Read annual reports of customers and competitors
- Attend competitor's webinars
- Read industry e-newsletters
- Listen to relevant podcasts
- Read business books
- Watch customer CEO media interviews
- Review customer service call logs
- Review product usage analytics

Discuss

Having periodic discussions with customers, internal teammates, and external parties gives you a ton of valuable information that you can ultimately use to help uncover customer problems. The conversations will help you learn about the immediate events that are happening and identify potential future market shifts that will impact your customers. It is important to learn about the industries in which you and your customers currently do business, as well as in global adjacent industries, so that you can make sense of the interconnectedness. For instance, the global automaker General Motors announced in early 2021 that they intend to phase out all gasoline and diesel motors in their passenger vehicles by the year 2035.[1] If your customer is in the oil and gas industry, they will certainly be paying close attention to that plan, and you should too.

Customer Discussions

"There is no justification for not talking to your customers," Zaid, a senior product manager at a Fortune 500 company, quipped as we were discussing how to best gather good feedback on customer needs. He continued, "I used to do situational discovery . . . I would gather feedback at a point in time early in a project and then move on to other activities. As I matured as a product manager, I realized the importance of continuously understanding your customers." Zaid further remarked, "I always insist on talking to customers directly as much as possible, because when I ask the questions and hear the answers first-hand, I can pick up on nuances that I wouldn't get otherwise. I take advantage of internal teammates who have insights on customers, but I always try to stay directly connected to customers."

There is much written about how to best "interview" customers. In my experience, the more an interaction looks and feels like an interview, the less fruitful the interaction is. The more you can make it a comfortable discussion during which you ask probing questions but are mostly an active listener, the more apt the customer will be to share real information.

Honing this skill is very important. One technique that helps sharpen it is a variation of the "Five Whys" method, an interrogative tool traditionally used to explore the cause-and-effect relationships of an issue. The method is part of the Toyota Production System, and was developed by Sakichi Toyoda, a Japanese inventor and industrialist. Taiichi Ohno (1912–1990), the architect of the Toyota Production System, once said, "the basis of Toyota's scientific approach is to ask *why* five times whenever we find a problem. . . . By repeating *why* five times, the nature of the problem as well as its solution becomes clear."[2]

The Toyota welding robot example is a classic:

1. **"Why did the robot stop?**
   The circuit was overloaded, causing a fuse to blow.
2. **"Why is the circuit overloaded?**
   There was insufficient lubrication on the bearings, so they locked up.
3. **"Why was there insufficient lubrication on the bearings?**
   The oil pump on the robot is not circulating sufficient oil.
4. **"Why is the pump not circulating sufficient oil?**
   The pump intake is clogged with metal shavings.
5. **"Why is the intake clogged with metal shavings?**
   Because there is no filter on the pump."[3]

I love the principle of this technique for extracting information from customers. You do not need to ask only "why" questions or ask precisely five of them. The point is to not take each answer as final; keep probing until you find valuable pieces of information.

As an example, Sheryl is a product manager for a fintech software company whose products allow small e-commerce websites to accept credit card payments. Liselotte is an entrepreneur who sells hand-made soaps and bath salts on her website. She uses Sheryl's product to accept payments on the site. Here is how a conversation between them might go:

Sheryl: *Hi, Liselotte. How have you been? How's business?*

Liselotte: *Hi! Business is great. Very busy. Our sales are up 35 percent from last year.*

Sheryl: *That's great. Is there anything you'd like to improve on?*

Liselotte: *Well, I'm trying to figure out how to reduce the number of people whose cards are getting declined. I seem to have people who are interested in buying, but they must not have the credit available.*

Sheryl: *Hmm. That's interesting. Tell me more about what you've found.*

Liselotte: *I don't know a lot. But it seems like they tend to be people from Canada.*

Sheryl: *Oh, okay. When we set you up a couple of years ago, weren't you only selling in the United States? You've expanded to Canada since then?*

Liselotte: *Yes, I have started to advertise to consumer targets in Canada, and I may start targeting other countries too.*

Sheryl: *Okay, that may be an easy fix. Let me check on your risk and fraud parameters.*

It turned out that Liselotte's account had been set up to flag and decline any transaction sent from outside of the United States. Sheryl not only discovered an immediate fix to improve the product for Liselotte but also learned more about her future expansion goals. Always be on the lookout for nuggets of insight that help you raise your customer intelligence.

Internal Teammate Discussions

Many insights come from our internal teammates. The folks around us usually have a great deal of industry expertise and gain valuable insights from their interactions with customers and others in the market. Consistent communication with various internal groups can shed light on many important matters. Be sure to carve out time to discuss more than just day-to-day product issues. Often, especially with those teammates closest to our daily work—engineering or sales, for example—we get so mired in the ongoing fire drills and standard operations that we neglect the important discussions that lead to deeper customer and market awareness. Set aside time to talk about industry trends, future technology predictions, and other forward-looking conversations.

Sales and Account Management

If you work in an organization with a salesforce, those folks have daily interactions with customers and prospects. They hear the perceived positives and negatives about your current products, ongoing needs of the customer base, and other market trends. If you are a global company, your regional representatives can share a great deal about local culture, regulations, and trends.

Corporate Strategy or Business Leadership

Many large companies have corporate strategy groups whose role is to research big trends and help set the path forward for the business. This research is invaluable to you as a product manager.

If you have this function in your company, become the group members' best friend. Talk with them often.

If your company does not have a dedicated strategy group, it does this work at various levels of the organization, either at the business unit level or at the company's executive level. Get to know the various business unit heads or the executives in your company. Have conversations with them often about what they are seeing and how it is driving their thoughts on the future.

Engineering and Design

Your engineering teammates are experts in the technology, science, structures, and systems that bring your products to life. They are also domain specialists with a deep curiosity about the world around them. I have always relied on my engineering partners to help teach me about current and future technologies that impact the customers and the business.

Your design partners are the ones who will be able to share trends in user experience, industrial design, accessibility, customer behavior, design inclusivity, and other important information that can help you better understand your customers.

Finance

Talk to your finance teammates about the financial results of your product, such as how the company accounts for and allocates costs to the product and the reporting level of the profit and loss. These folks often also have a good sense for which big market trends and global economic movements are likely to impact the business. This can be important information as you are thinking about your product's future.

Customer Service

Customer service groups talk to customers every day. The representatives can give you great insights into issues customers are having and the overall product experience. Sitting in on customer service calls or chats is incredibly valuable. Reviewing the data logs across customer interactions can also illuminate future problems you may be able to solve.

Operations

Depending on your organization, the operations group may look quite different. In software companies, these folks may be doing DevOps work to ensure the technology on which products are built, tested, and deployed is efficient and stable. They may also handle customer onboarding or internal processes and develop tools for attracting and retaining employees. In durable or physical goods companies, these teams are responsible for supply chain organization, capacity planning, vendor management, and manufacturing. They may also be responsible for creating packaging and producing product displays. In services companies, these teams are often responsible for customer onboarding and maintaining supporting technology platforms such as communications and project management tools. Talking to these teammates about trends in customer experience, tools, processes, and even talent management can be fruitful for some of the things your customers may be going through.

Let me make an important point here about gleaning customer insights from these conversations: do not completely "outsource" customer interaction to internal partners. Sometimes, from both a time and a comfort level perspective, it is easier to talk to internal teammates than it is to talk to customers. But you still must talk to customers—a lot! Leverage your internal teammates, but realize that each has their own perspective. The salesperson's job is to support the account and incentivize the customer to buy more of your existing products. The operations person's job may be to help a customer with the mechanics of implementing or using the product. Both are important activities for the business, but talking directly to customers is the most critical way to dig deep into the customers' longer-term goals and plans, and that is the product manager's responsibility.

External Discussions

No matter how knowledgeable we and our colleagues are, there is still the risk of only seeing the world as it exists within the four walls of our organization. Leveraging your external network helps fill in the full picture.

You likely have former coworkers at other companies in the industry. Keep in touch with them. Of course, do not share or solicit any proprietary information about your company or theirs, but discussing high-level happenings can be very fruitful for either confirming what you're seeing or identifying some areas you may need to dig deeper into your analysis.

Speaking with market analysts about the industry is always a good way to keep up with trends. And, attending industry events or even speaking at events with other industry leaders establishes relationships and communication channels for ongoing conversations.

All of these—customers, internal teammates, and external parties—are folks you should have discussions with on a consistent basis.

Here are some useful methods for discussing what is happening around you:

Observe

Sam, a product manager at a recruiting software company, was visiting with a large customer in their office in Chicago when he noticed a sticky note on a recruiter's computer monitor.

"What's that?" Sam asked.

"Oh, I can never remember how to navigate to the candidate page in the tool, so I just made myself a little note," the recruiter answered.

"Wow, so it's a little difficult to get there?"

"It's okay, I just needed a little help."

"Why didn't you bring that up when we were chatting last month about how it was going with the product?" Sam inquired.

"Eh, it's not that big of a deal. I didn't really think about it."

But it was a big deal to Sam. He went back to the office and searched the customer service notes to see if there were other customers bringing this up. As it turned out, several customers had mentioned that it was a bit cumbersome getting to that part of the module. Sam worked with designers to find a quick, user-friendly way of getting to that page from the user's dashboard, and it was added to the next major release. A small change greatly impacted the customer experience. Sam would not have recognized this issue had he not been with the customer and seen the sticky note on the customer's monitor. Not everything is raised through our discussions. Often, we need to observe it ourselves.

Sometimes, we find more critical product issues when we observe customers interacting with products. A medical device company, for example, was working on an automated external defibrillator, a device that uses an electrical shock to restore the heart rhythm back to normal during a cardiac incident. The devices are designed to be used during a medical emergency in offices, group residences, or other public places by laypeople with no medical background. They are typically installed on a wall in an easily accessible place and are small and lightweight enough to be usable by most people—about 12 in. by 12 in. (30 cm. by 30 cm.) in size and roughly 5 lbs. (2 kg.) in weight.

During the design process, the medical device company's product team decided to remove the on/off power switch and instead have the device turn on as soon as someone removes it from the wall and opens it. Reasonably, the team thought that not having to turn on the device would save valuable seconds in an emergency. After creating a prototype of the device, the team set up a simulated emergency scenario in a commercial building with real office workers.

The workers knew only that the simulation involved a medical emergency with one of their colleagues and that they were to use the defibrillator to try to help their colleague. They were given no instructions on how to use the device other than those printed on the device itself.

As the designated person began having the simulated cardiac episode, the workers jumped up and grabbed the defibrillator from the wall. They started fumbling around trying to find the switch to turn the device on. It took them 13 seconds to realize the device was already on and ready to be used. A cardiac arrest victim's chance of survival drops about ten percent with each passing minute, so every second can literally mean the difference between life and death.[4]

What the product team thought would save time ended up adding critical seconds to the process. They would not have realized this without being on-site, observing the simulation with real people. The product team took their learnings and redesigned the unit with explicit step-by-step instructions that told the user the unit was on and ready to use.

Here are some useful methods you can use to observe the world around you:

OBSERVE Q

- Observe customers using your product
- Observe customers installing your product
- Tour customer factories
- Listen to customer service calls
- Analyze product usage pattern data
- Attend product demos
- Observe your customers' focus groups
- Reverse engineer competitor products

Customer intelligence is the bedrock of everything we do in product management. Without understanding who our customers are, what is driving them, and what problems they need solved, none of our work matters much.

KEY TAKEAWAYS

- Great product managers have an extremely high level of customer intelligence.
- Customer intelligence is made up of four key elements: customer characteristics; situations and market conditions; motivations and drivers; and pain points and unmet needs.
- Before building intelligence on your customers, clearly identify and articulate all the constituents in your customer chain: first-line, second-line, third-line, and end-user.
- The most consistent way to continuously build customer intelligence is to diligently study, discuss, and observe.

GREAT PRODUCT MANAGERS ARE EXPERTS AT BUILDING RELATIONSHIPS

Interpersonal relations involve human beings with varying emotions and personalities, and as such can be quite imprecise. There is no one perfect formula for building relationships that works for all people in all situations.

However, there is a tenet that underlies all great relationships between product managers and their teammates: confidence. Great product managers have:

1. earned the trust and confidence of their team, and
2. inspired a widespread belief in the product and its future.

When these two things are solid, relationships will be on good footing. If one of these is absent, the foundation of the relationship is shaky. If both are absent, there is very little chance for a productive working relationship.

> *Almost every successful person begins with two beliefs: the future can be better than the present, and I have the power to make it so.*
>
> —David Brooks

EARNING THE TEAM'S CONFIDENCE

A product manager I was coaching once asked me, "How do I convey my thoughts in a room of experts? Many engineers in my organization have bold opinions and strong personalities. How do I speak up, have my opinion heard, and inspire confidence?"

It is important to remember that you need not be an expert on everything to build credibility and trust. In fact, great product managers show vulnerability and are transparent about where their expertise lies and where they need to rely on their partners.

I am not a technical expert by education or experience. I have built and worked on technical products over my career, but my expertise has always been more on the market and business side. Earlier in my career, I tried very hard to fake my level of technical acumen, thinking that I had to be a technical expert or I would have no credibility. That did not work out so well. My engineering partners could easily tell I was in over my head trying to discuss the technical details. Once I was transparent about where I brought value and where I needed support from partners, the team was better able to leverage each other's strengths and build trust among the group. I could not lay out the technical options, but I could bring the customer perspective and business ramifications to team discussions. My credibility grew as I became more realistic and transparent about my strengths and weaknesses. Be confident in your strengths and transparent in where others' strengths are needed.

Additionally, it is difficult to work successfully as a team if some of the teammates do not buy into the current viability and future vision of the product. Few things derail good relationships as much as misaligned expectations do. Product teams must be on the same page when it comes to where the product is going and why. As a product manager, you should have a vision for where you want the product to go. The vision should be built in collaboration with the team and be steadfast, clear, and easily communicated. The details of how to execute on the vision should be malleable, but the vision itself should be firm.

Teammates will have confidence in you as a product manager when you display the customer knowledge, business wisdom, and judgment to make good decisions for the product and set a vision rooted in that knowledge, wisdom, and judgment. People want to work on products that can make a difference for customers. Great product managers foster a belief that the team can achieve great things.

Confidence does not happen by magic, of course. It grows from a consistent dedication to collaboration, open communication, and empathy. It is built one conversation, one solved problem, one vulnerable moment, one success, and even one misstep at a time. Transactional confidence builds up over time until you have real, lasting trust in one another.

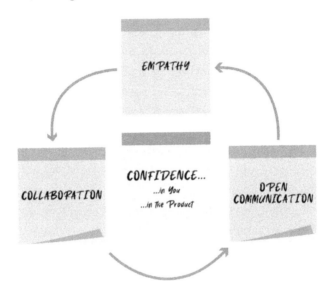

Collaboration

If you want to go fast, go alone. If you want to go far, go together.

—African Proverb

I am a golfer. I played a lot of competitive golf in my younger years and even played in college at Texas Tech University (go Red Raiders!). One of the things I love about golf is that it is an individual sport. If I am going to succeed on the golf course, it is up to me and only me. I cannot rely on someone else to hit the shot or make the putt for me. I relish that autonomy and even the pressure that comes with it.

Product management is not an individual sport. No one person can hit all the shots or make all the putts. It is more like baseball, a team sport in which each teammate plays an interconnected role and the collective performance of the individual roles determine success.

Product management brings together a team of people, all with different skill sets and perspectives, who work in tandem to identify the right problem and then solve it in the most creative, feasible, and valuable way. Those different skill sets and perspectives across the team provide a key component of collaboration. Viewing a situation through different lenses illuminates diverse life experiences, breeds more empathy and understanding, and brings varying ideas to the table.

Once, I was chit-chatting with a coworker and the topic of pet peeves came up. I began lamenting about people who did not return their shopping carts (buggies, trolleys) to the designated return area at the supermarket. I was incredulous and sure this showed an irreparable character flaw. How could anyone be so lazy as to not just take it the few hundred feet back to the return?

"Yeah, lots of people feel that way," my coworker laughed. "But let me share another perspective," she said.

> I have two small children, both still needing to be secured in car seats. Once I get the kids in their seats, I do not want to leave them alone while I return the cart. I know it is only a few moments, but I don't feel comfortable leaving them. I try to put the cart in the best place where it will be out of the way, but I do not return it all the way to the corral or store.

Another coworker heard the conversation and came over to join in:

> When I had my knee surgery, I was on crutches for a while. I had to go shopping one day and they didn't have any of the riding carts, so I stumbled along on my crutches pushing the cart as best I could. When I got out to the parking lot, I couldn't muster the energy to get the cart back to the store, so I just left it by my car. I had always been one of those "good people return the cart; evil people leave them in the parking lot" kinds of people. No in between. Turns out, it is not that cut and dry.

Well, didn't I feel like an arse?

I am a childless, able-bodied woman and had never considered others' extenuating circumstances. I learned a valuable lesson to be sensitive to other perspectives and recognize that one person's reality is not everyone's.

That is why collaboration is so important to the relationships within your product ecosystem. True collaboration is when varying perspectives, ideas, experiences, and opinions come together to challenge the status quo, look at things creatively, and determine together the best path forward.

Open Communication

Speaking directly and openly even if it may create conflict is difficult for many people, myself included. By the way, conflict is in the eye of the beholder, so what rises to the level of conflict may be different for you than for one of your teammates. Perhaps you think conflict is reserved for those situations when there is a good dose of yelling and screaming. I think conflict is asking something that causes even the slightest inconvenience to the other person. For as long as I can remember, I have avoided conflict, which is quite wearing while having such a low threshold of what constitutes conflict!

One time when I was about 11 years old, I was at a friend's house eating breakfast with her family. We had silver dollar pancakes—you know, those ones that are only a couple of inches wide and the size of a silver dollar coin. Tiny food is so fun. Anyway, the syrup bottle was across the table, out of my reach. I wanted syrup, but I was afraid to speak up and ask for it. I distinctly remember thinking, *I should just ask. But they would offer it to me if they thought I should have it. Maybe it's rude to ask. I'll just eat them plain.* My heart was literally racing over this internal struggle. How in the world does asking someone to pass the syrup become a conflict? Well, that is just my quirky personality, I guess. Thankfully, I have become a bit more outspoken in my adult years; you will be glad to know I can painlessly ask for the syrup now.

Some of you may have similar struggles and avoid conflict at all costs. Others of you may be quite comfortable with conflict. If you are like me, you may need to be very diligent in building this ability. For those of you who do not break out in sweats at the thought of making a simple request, realize that not everyone is like you. You may need to throttle your directness a bit as you get to know people. Respect for various personalities goes a long way in relationship building.

But here is the thing: open, direct communication is a bedrock of successful relationships, so no matter how difficult it may be for some of us, we must build this strength. Being direct does not mean being blunt or rude. It means being clear and straightforward about what we need and what is expected of each other. The best work relationships are between people who can openly and constructively challenge each other in a way that generates new ideas and new ways of doing things. In Adam Grant's book *Think Again*, he discusses the importance that conflict can have for high-performing teams. He specifically talks about the difference between "relationship conflict" and "task conflict."[5] Relationship conflict encompasses personal, emotional battles about ideas or opinions. Task conflict entails debating over how to best accomplish something. As you can imagine, relationship conflict is not constructive and often even destructive, while task conflict can be quite beneficial.

I have seen this first-hand in my work with organizations. When I am conducting a workshop with a group of coworkers from a company, I often start the session with a generic, "Feel free to interact with each other, discuss the findings across the teams, and ask questions if you have them." I intentionally do not instruct them to "question each other" or anything of the sort. I want to see their natural interaction patterns. The best teams are those that can comfortably challenge and probe others' theories and engage in active dialogue about how something might work best. When I see the groups do this, I know they have relationships that allow for the type of interaction that holds everyone accountable for bringing their best ideas and work to the table.

Empathy

Empathy is the ability to sense other people's emotions, put yourself in their shoes, and imagine how they feel. It is a powerful and important ability for product managers. When you can genuinely have empathy for customers and for your internal teammates, you will connect with them on a deeper level.

Without realizing it at the time, I learned a lot about empathy and its importance to relationships from my mother, Paula, who owned a flower shop for over 30 years. Flowerland Florist & Gifts, or "the shop" as we called it, was an integral part of my life growing up.

"No one needs flowers," Paula would often say. I remember as a kid wondering how a business whose products customers do not even need could survive. I learned what Paula meant when I would see customers come in to buy flowers for the funeral of their loved one who had just died. It was one of the worst days of their lives. So many customers literally cried on her shoulder. They did not need the flowers. They needed the shoulder. Paula knew that.

She was there during the best and worst times of her customers' lives, including weddings, new babies, birthdays, illnesses, and funerals. Toward the end of Paula's career, before she sold Flowerland, the competitive landscape had dramatically changed. People could buy flowers at grocery stores, big-box warehouse stores, gas stations, and over the internet. Yet many still went to Flowerland to buy flowers because Paula saw them as humans first and customers second.

See your coworkers as humans first. Of course, the work you do together is important, and you will have expectations of each other. But showing empathy in the workplace involves understanding what is happening not only in the job but also outside of work. Not everyone is comfortable sharing personal details of their lives, but rest assured, everyone has things going on in their personal lives that are impacting them either positively or negatively. There is nothing necessarily for you to do about things happening outside of work, but simply be sensitive and kind.

> *Everyone you know is fighting a battle you know nothing about. Be kind. Always.*
>
> —Brad Meltzer

ASSESSING YOUR RELATIONSHIPS

Your Product Ecosystem

An ecosystem is a biological community of interacting organisms and their physical environment. Product managers work within a product management ecosystem, a community of interacting functions and the organizational infrastructure designed to support a business' products. Strong relationships with teammates in the ecosystem are critical for any product manager. Just like natural ecosystems, product management ecosystems are dynamic and fluid and are influenced by both external and internal factors. The relationships within should also be actively managed to ensure long-term sustainability of products and services.

The people in your ecosystem are those who participate in or lead activities involving your products. Who brings ideas to the table? Who scopes and validates ideas with you? Who funds the product? Who designs the product? Who creates the user experience? Who develops, sources, or manufactures the product? Who prices, sells, markets, and supports the product? The answers to those questions indicate the teammates with whom you need to sustain productive relationships.

You may work in an environment that has dedicated product teams. Maybe you call them pods, squads, or a team of missionaries. Maybe they are a scrum team, a Kanban team, or an innovation team. The semantics abound. This primary product team typically includes a product manager, a user experience designer, a product designer, and engineers. Occasionally, there is also a product marketer, scrum master, or business analyst in this team. This team is responsible for the day-to-day activities of the product, and these are the folks you work with most closely. For simplicity, I refer to this as the core product team. Your product ecosystem is bigger than just your core product team, however. It also includes others who may not be involved with your daily routine but are nonetheless integral to the product's success. These people include those in sales, marketing, finance, and operations. As a product manager, you need to establish relationships with everyone in your ecosystem. Some relationships may be more important than others, but you ultimately need visibility and rapport with everyone who plays a part in your product's success.

PRODUCT ECOSYSTEM

OPERATIONS
- Support
- Manufacturing
- Supply Chain
- Product Operations
- Product Analytics
- Internal IT

SALES
- Inside Sales
- Direct Sales
- Customer Success
- Account Management
- External Agents
- Brokers

CORE PRODUCT TEAM
- Product Management
- User Experience
- Product Design
- Engineering
- Product Marketing

FINANCE
- Planning & Analysis
- Financial Reporting
- Budgeting
- Pricing
- Actuarial
- Risk Management

MARKETING
- Content
- Branding
- Events
- Social Media
- Communication

Building relationships with the people who are important to your product requires making an organized, purposeful plan. You cannot "process your way" through human interactions, but you can—and should—commit to a plan that identifies which relationships are important, the state of each relationship, and a plan of action for establishing, improving, or nurturing each relationship. Remember, great product managers do not leave things as important as cross-functional relationships to chance.

You can use a relationship map to represent all the people who are in your product ecosystem. If you are new to the position, you may need to ask your manager, peers, or others to help you identify the people involved with your product. If you have been in the role for a while, you likely already know who will be on your map, but it is still an important exercise to depict them all in one clear picture.

Depending on the size of your organization, you will likely end up with between six and 20 people on your map. Some will be more critical to your day-to-day work, and others will be more ancillary in their interactions with you. All are important in their own way, and some people may be included in more than one of the categories.

If you do not have a dedicated group member for a specific function, then put the manager of that group on your map and work to have a relationship with them. For instance, it is helpful to have a good rapport with the finance group for times when you need help with product pricing, risk management, or obtaining your product's financial data. There may not, however, be one dedicated person in the finance group who is assigned to work specifically with your product; rather, when a need arises, any of the people in the group may help. In this case, it is usually best to establish a relationship with the finance manager or equivalent role that oversees those people who are most likely to pitch in on your requests. Additionally, when you work with someone from that group on a project, make sure you get to know them as best as possible so you have a friendly teammate in the group.

What is not necessary to add to your relationship map is anyone who does not have material impact on the product. For example, as an employee of the company, you may want to have a relationship with the human resources manager. But that person is not someone who works on the product and as such is not in your product ecosystem.

RELATIONSHIP MAP

For Your Product, Who Helps...

IDEATE	SCOPE/VALIDATE	DESIGN PRODUCT

DESIGN UX	DEVELOP/SOURCE	PRICE

MARKET/PROMOTE	SELL	SUPPORT

FUND	PROVIDE DATA	OTHER...

Relationship Status

Once you have added everyone to your relationship map, plot each one on a relationship status chart. This will help you visualize the current state of your relationships so you can set a plan for each one.

The Y axis on the relationship status chart is your level of credibility with that person. In other words, does the person have confidence in your ability as a product manager? The X axis is that person's belief in the product. That is, how strongly does that person believe in the product and the go-forward vision for it?

For each person on your relationship map, assign a score of 0 to 3 for how confident they are in you as the product manager and assign a score of 0 to 3 for their confidence in the product itself. Then plot each person on the chart according to their score.

What is important here is to be as honest as you can on these assessments. Admitting that someone believes you have little credibility is not easy. And frankly, even if you do not agree with them, it is their perception that matters. At least for this exercise, perception is reality. If someone has little confidence in you, you will have to work to change that perception, so that will be part of your relationship plan for them.

This exercise is sometimes done collaboratively, meaning you can ask people to plot themselves on the chart. Again, you may need to have thick skin if someone plots themselves in a way that is not flattering to you or your product.

You must have the actual, real picture before you can do anything to improve it. If you or someone in your product ecosystem sugarcoats the current state, that state will remain or even worsen. Bite the bullet and learn the truth. Even if it hurts for a while.

The rating scale:

- **Y Axis: Confidence in Product Manager (i.e., Does this person see you as credible in the product manager role?)**
  - **0 = None.** These people do not know you well enough to have formed an opinion about your ability as a product manager. If you are new to the

role, you may plot most people here because no one really knows you yet. If they are new to their role, they may have not had a chance to work with you closely enough yet.

- ○ **1 = Low.** These folks perceive you as somewhat credible but believe you have much room for improvement.
- ○ **2 = Medium.** These people have confidence in you. You have proven yourself in their eyes. There is some room for improvement, but they believe you are credible and can get the job done.
- ○ **3 = High.** These are the people who have almost total confidence in you. They have seen you shine and will go to bat for you.

- **X Axis: Confidence in Product (i.e., Does this person believe in the product itself and the vision for its future?)**
  - ○ **0 = Unclear.** These folks have not yet had a chance to hear about the product and the product vision or are still unclear about them. They have not dismissed or embraced the product but need more information to form an opinion.
  - ○ **1 = Skeptic.** These people do not believe in the product or the vision for its future. They may not believe in the viability of the product itself, have misgivings about the go-forward plan, or both.
  - ○ **2 = Accept.** These are the people who accept the product as sustainable and the vision as workable. There may be room for more enthusiasm, but they generally believe the product has merit.
  - ○ **3 = Support.** These folks fully support the product and believe the vision is the best path forward for it.

RELATIONSHIP STATUS CHART

Once you plot a person on the chart, they will fall into a category that indicates the current state of your relationship with them. They will be a champion, an ally, a passive advocate, a detractor, or new.

Champion
These folks understand your vision and have a positive, established relationship with you. They will be the ones to fight for your product in the organization and with customers. You will obviously want to have some champions. Even if you do not have any now, your goal is to establish a few champion relationships.

Ally
These are people who have confidence in your abilities, but they have not yet bought into the product. This may be because they do not know enough about it or because

they are skeptical about the validity of the product or the vision for the product.

Passive Advocate

These are people with whom you may not yet have a personal relationship, but they believe in the product itself. They see the value in the product, they believe there is a strong market for it, and they think the organization can achieve success with the product. They are likely not the ones to proactively tout the product (or you) around the organization, but when asked about it, they emit positivity and advocacy.

In some cases, you may have someone who believes in the product vision but has a bad relationship with you for some reason, so you will need to address that.

Detractor

These are people who have openly expressed their lack of belief in the product's worth or disagreed with the vision and plan for the product's future. Perhaps they have their own ideas about where the product should go or have not bought into the organization's ability to execute the plan for the product.

Detractors also view your credibility as low. In their eyes, you have not proven your ability. These are the most difficult relationships, and sometimes you must meet uncomfortable conflict head-on. There may even be a personal conflict you must work out.

New

You have no relationship with these people, and they have not yet formed an opinion of you or the product. They are likely new to the company or team, or you are new to the product manager role.

Let's look at an example. Spalding is a product manager at an enterprise software company and has assigned the following scores to the teammates on his relationship map:

NAME	ROLE	CONFIDENCE IN PM	BELIEF IN PRODUCT
ALEX	Engineer	2	1
PIPER	Product Marketing Manager	3	2
KNOX	Senior Sales Manager	1	3
QUINN	Engineering Manager	0	1
SAWYER	Financial Analyst	0	0

RELATIONSHIP STATUS CHART EXAMPLE

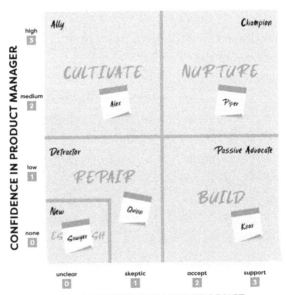

Alex is an ally. She has a good working relationship with Spalding and believes in his abilities, but she does not consider the product to be a viable solution for the long term. Alex has made it known that she believes the company should get out of this product type and move on to other opportunities with higher growth potential. Spalding can leverage the personal credibility he has with Alex to try to sway her on the product's vision.

Piper is a champion. He has absolute confidence in Spalding's ability to lead the product team and orchestrate it for success. Piper also accepts that the product vision is one that has proven to be solid and will continue leading to success. Spalding will nurture this relationship with Piper to ensure it remains strong. He may also enlist Piper to help advocate for him and for the product vision with other teammates.

Knox is a passive advocate. He strongly believes in the product and the vision for its future. He thinks Spalding is somewhat credible but has not worked with him long enough to build a high level of trust. Spalding will try to build a relationship with Knox and convert him into a champion.

Quinn is a detractor. She is new to the engineering manager role, so she does not know Spalding well enough to have an opinion about his abilities. However, during her short term in the role, she has been influenced by Alex's view on the limited practicality of the product. Spalding will need to repair this relationship by creating a personal rapport with Quinn and trying to sway her on the product's future prospects.

Sawyer is new to the team, so he has no relationship with Spalding or understanding of the product. Spalding will need to establish a relationship with him.

NAME	ROLE	CONFIDENCE IN PM	BELIEF IN PRODUCT	RELATIONSHIP STATUS	RELATIONSHIP PLAN
ALEX	Engineer	2	1	Ally	Cultivate
PIPER	Product Marketing Manager	3	2	Champion	Nurture
KNOX	Senior Sales Manager	1	3	Passive Advocate	Build
QUINN	Engineering Manager	0	1	Detractor	Repair
SAWYER	Financial Analyst	0	0	New	Establish

RELATIONSHIP PLANS

As you begin a journey to enhance relationships, remember two things:

1. Your relationships in product management are constructed upon two main elements: confidence in you and confidence in the product. Your work on building the other truths of customer intelligence, communication, judgment, and prioritization, as well as naturally gaining more experience as time goes on, will help create a foundation for good relationships because doing so helps build belief in you and in the product.
2. People are different, so it will take some personalization to build each relationship. There is no one-size-fits-all when it comes to relationship building. Remember to embrace collaboration, open communication, and empathy as you are getting to know each person.

Establish

Starting from scratch to build a relationship gives you the opportunity to start off on the right foot. You do not yet know much about each other, so you need to first introduce yourselves and establish the very basics of the relationship.

Once when I was new at a company, I created an "About Me" slide that I used to introduce myself to the team in our first team meeting. I then asked each person to do the same and share with the team at the next meeting. I included information about where I was from, my career background, how I typically like to work (call, email, asynchronous preferences), my family, pictures of my cats, and something interesting about me. I tried to make it light and fun. This seemed to break the ice, and each person enjoyed sharing about themselves in the next team meeting. Not only did I learn about my new teammates, but they each learned something new about each other, even though they'd been working together for a while. It helped with the team camaraderie. Once the team shared together, I then had a base on which to begin building one-on-one relationships with each person. It is important to keep in mind that some people like to share, and some people are quite private, so be respectful of what you expect others to share with you or the team.

Sometimes establishing a relationship starts with simply having coffee or lunch together. If you are not located in the same place, a virtual get-to-know-you session can substitute. Talk about yourselves and discuss the roles each of you play on the team.

Here are some questions that may help you begin establishing a relationship:

- Tell me about your role. Who do you work with mostly on a day-to-day basis?
- What is your favorite part of the company?
- What made you want to join the company / move to this role?
- Do you know anything about the product yet? If so, what do you think?
- Any advice for me as I am getting started?

Build

To further develop a relationship with a teammate, use your shared belief in a product to create a bond. Talk about the product and the mutual work you do on the product. Ask about their priorities, what their boss has asked of them, and how they see their role in the product ecosystem. Remember, these folks will have some level of confidence in the product but have yet to form a real trust in you as the product manager. So, have open conversations about what they expect from you and what you expect from them. Hash out differences in expectations. The only way to get past issues is to directly address them.

Cultivate

With the teammates who already believe in you, focus on leveraging that trust to improve their confidence level in the product. This often comes down to sharing more about the problem you are solving and why you think it is a valuable problem to focus on. Sharing the story of the customer—who they are and how this problem impacts them—is also a good way to build belief in the product. Sometimes the person may believe it is a problem worth solving but thinks the solution you have chosen is not viable or optimal. In this case, listen to their concerns, try to persuade them, or even take some of their advice. They may have very valid points about the solution, and if you show that you can take guidance for the betterment of the product, it can go a long way toward building a strong relationship. Of course, the team must ultimately all agree it is a good direction, but you should keep an open mind as you are discussing these issues.

Nurture

Nurture your champions. They already believe in you and the product. Nurturing these relationships simply entails ensuring you are keeping in touch, sharing news, listening to what is going on with them, and generally upkeeping the relationship. Ask them for help when you need it. Offer support when they need you. Do not take these relationships for granted; your champions will be your strongest advocates.

Repair

Repairing is the most difficult part of relationships. You and your teammates may have many differences, and it can be easy to focus on those. However, you will likely have one thing in common, and that is the desire to work on a successful product and with a successful team. Use that as the starting point for repairing these relationships.

The first step here is to ask these teammates to clearly articulate why they have little confidence in you and in the product. These will not be easy conversations, but they are necessary. Be clear that you want to repair the relationship so that you can work better together and build a better product in the end. Ask them to be as open and honest—but respectful, of course—as possible.

Lay out each issue between you and clarify the details of each. For example, if they say something like, "You do not seem to ever meet your deliverables to the team," ask for specific examples. It is important to not be defensive. Remember, at this point you are not trying to prove them wrong in their perception, but simply lay out the issues that must be overcome.

After you have discussed and are clear on each issue, commit to each other that you will work on them. You will not be able to repair this relationship overnight, so be clear about what you want to do and set realistic expectations of each other.

One last thing: I always suggest having these tough conversations one-on-one with the person whose relationship needs repairing. We are all adults and need to be able to hash things out in a productive way. However, if the situation has become so untenable that a one-on-one meeting would not be productive or psychologically safe, ask your boss and the other person's boss to participate.

KEY TAKEAWAYS

- Great product managers are experts at building relationships.
- The relationships product managers have with their teammates are typically influenced by two key drivers: confidence in you as the product manager and confidence in the product.
- List each person in your product ecosystem on a relationship map.
- Assess your relationships and plot each one on a relationship status chart.
- Devise an appropriate plan to establish, build, cultivate, nurture, or repair the relationships with those in your product ecosystem.

GREAT PRODUCT MANAGERS ARE MASTER COMMUNICATORS

Good communication is the bridge between confusion and clarity.

—Nat Turner

Communication is an inherent part of product management. Whether debating product direction, sharing market knowledge, translating technical jargon into customer-friendly language, providing updates to leadership, or giving direct feedback to peers, good communication is key to maintaining clarity and context about the myriad activities surrounding the product.

Great product managers become master communicators by focusing on two imperatives: connection and clarity. Communication is meaningless if our messages are ambiguous or do not connect with the audience.

CONNECTION

Communication is one of the most important methods of human connection. But communication alone does not guarantee connection. We can talk to someone about the weather or the local sports team for half an hour, and even quite enjoy the conversation, but we may still have no real bond with them. Great product managers embrace the idea that to be successful in their inherently cross-functional work, there must be an authentic connection among teammates. Good product managers inform. Great product managers connect.

We have all known someone who we would consider a "people person"—a gregarious, life-of-the-party type who easily builds rapport with others. Many product managers have this personality. But many product managers are quiet, reserved types who find group and social interactions challenging. I have learned over my career that extroverts, introverts, and ambiverts can all become master communicators and connect deeply with those around them.

Three skills help you better connect with others: storytelling, intentional listening, and adapting to the audience.

Storytelling

Product managers are awash in various facts about their products: retention rate, customer satisfaction score, monthly recurring revenue, active user statistics, inventory levels, supplier lead times, and on and on. While data is important, the stories behind the data evoke much greater emotion. Facts and figures activate two parts of your brain while stories activate seven, which more fully engages the brain and triggers memorable, positive emotions.[6] Everyone in the product ecosystem must connect with the customer, and stories are a powerful vehicle for promoting that connection.

All good stories include five components: characters, setting, plot, conflict, and resolution. Product stories are no different. It is important to note that while we call this a product story, it is really about your customer. Your customer only cares about your product in the context that it can solve a problem for them. Otherwise, it is meaningless to them. Your product would not exist if it were not for your customer. A product story is the story of your customer. To craft your story, hearken back to the information you compiled as you were building your level of customer intelligence.

1. **Characters**: The main characters of your story are your customers. You will likely need a separate story for each of the customers in your customer chain.
2. **Setting**: This is where the story takes place. It includes the industries and geographies in which your business customers

do business or the geographies in which your individual customers live and work.

3. **Plot**: This is the crux of what is happening for your customers. It includes trends in the market, the business impact of those trends, the competitive landscape, issues with employment, and so on.

4. **Conflict**: This is the problem your customer faces.

5. **Resolution**: This is where your product may come into the story. How does the product solve the customer's problems? If your product does not yet address the problems, you may want to discuss how, or if, the customer currently addresses the problems with other solutions. If there are no real solutions yet, you may not have a well-defined resolution.

Example of a Product Story

Tasha has been working as an in-house recruiter for Enterprise Financial Software, Inc. (EFSI) for over eight years and has never seen the pace at which they are currently hiring. A flourishing tech company, EFSI was started ten years ago in Seattle by a human resources manager turned software engineer. Tasha has become accustomed to the continuous hiring cycle at a growing tech company, but EFSI has just opened its first location in Europe, and she is now responsible for hiring all the engineering and product talent for that location. In addition, the "great resignation" trend has hit the company, and many employees are finding greener pastures outside the company, pushing employee turnover up to almost 25 percent. Tasha has gone from managing about 30 open jobs to over 60 at any given time!

Though the number of applicants for the job openings has increased, Tasha is still having problems filling the roles, largely because of the offered salary ranges. Average wages across EFSI's industry have been soaring, but the company's leadership has yet to embrace a change in pay scales and benefits. Every day, Tasha loses a candidate because they instead choose opportunities with better compensation packages.

On one hand, Tasha loves seeing candidates have more leverage in negotiations because she has always seen herself as a champion of employees over corporations. Even though she technically works for "The Man," she takes great pride in her role of helping people further their career goals. But she has a job to do for the company, and one of her performance metrics is closing job requisitions within four weeks of the job posting. Tasha has been falling short on that goal, averaging over seven weeks to fill spots. This is the first time in her career that she has not met her performance goals, which is really impacting her esteem and enthusiasm. That, coupled with the fact that she has more than doubled her workload, has Tasha understandably burned out.

Oh, and did I mention that her kids are now back to attending virtual school from home because of the latest COVID variant outbreak? So, she is working twice as much, helping both kids with virtual school, and wondering if 10 a.m. is too early to start drinking wine.

While things are certainly stressful for Tasha, one bright spot has been a new way of finding viable candidates from nontraditional backgrounds. These are folks who may not have otherwise passed the first resume screening. Over the past month, she has placed seven such candidates who have not only proven to be qualified but also brought a refreshing perspective to the team.

A few notes about product stories are important to remember:

- If a story is crafted well, you may not even recognize that a product is in it. The example above focuses on a recruiting software company whose product has a predictive analytics algorithm built on finding candidates with underlying skills and qualities, even if they do not meet the traditional experience threshold. You get a glimpse of that in the end (the resolution), but the bulk of the story is about Tasha.

- You may not be able or willing to solve all the customer's problems, but it is still important to lay out the full picture of the customer. The recruiting software that helped Tasha find nontraditional candidates is not necessarily addressing the issue of leadership refusing to increase compensation, but it is still an important element to the story because it adds to her stress.

- You more often tell your product story verbally, but it may be quite helpful to write it out, read it aloud to colleagues, get feedback, and edit until you get the full story.

Intentional Listening

Have you ever been talking to someone, nodding and staring right at them, uttering occasional affirmations, knowing full well that you have not really heard a single word they said? Yeah, me too. My wife loves that.

Do not do that with your teammates (or spouse). Intentional listening is a method of listening with the explicit intent of connecting with the other person. The aspects of intentional listening do not always come naturally to everyone, so it can take some practice to get good at it. Intentional listening requires the following four habits:

1) **Avoid making it about you.** Remember, this is not about merely informing; it is about connecting. Rarely do one-sided conversations connect. You must be willing to give over control, at least for part of the conversation. A common trap is projecting

yourself into someone's story. When someone shares something with you, it is natural to want to commiserate by sharing something similar that happened to you. It may seem counterintuitive not to do this, but it rarely adds to the connection. In fact, doing so can disengage the other person. It is not about you at the moment, so keep the conversation centered on them.

2) **Hold space for the other person.** Holding space for someone means being available and emotionally present for them. It may be as substantial as clearing a couple of hours on your calendar or as simple as putting your phone away to show that you are fully present. When you hold space for someone, your only role is to provide a safe, supportive place for sharing. Avoid going into problem-solving mode; holding space is about only listening and supporting.

3) **Display innocuous curiosity.** This is very different from inserting your endless questions into the conversation (which often comes across as making it about you). Innocuous curiosity is a genuine interest in learning more about the person or topic. Asking questions such as "Tell me more about that," or "Oh, what was that like?" or "How did that make you feel?" disarm the other person and help them open up.

4) **Confirm what you heard.** This entails restating what you think you heard in your own words so that you confirm that you understand. We deal with complex issues in product management, so sometimes we need to translate from one "functional language" to another. For example, if you are a product manager without a technical background, you may not fully understand the technical jargon. That is okay, but you need to ensure that you get what it means to the user.

> Engineer: *We are having some latency issues because our encrypted connections are not optimized.*
>
> You: *Okay, so basically the user is seeing some delays in connecting to our app?*

Even if no real "translation" is needed—because you understand the technical jargon, for example—it is best practice to still confirm what you hear to ensure cohesion.

Adapting to Your Audience

Like most product managers, you have likely been in a meeting with your engineering team discussing the minutiae of features, and then in your very next meeting you had to flip a switch and talk high-level strategy with the leadership team. Great product managers can quickly pivot and adapt their message to the interests of the audience.

MESSAGE CONTINUUM

Audience Point of View/Interest

low   medium   high

Level of Detail Needed in Message

The information that internal teammates care about typically comes down to three matters: why, what, and how—*why* something should be done in the first place, *what* we should do about it, and *how* we will do it. Great product managers adapt their message and associated level of detail to meet their audience's point of view.

Here are some questions and tips to consider for adapting to a stakeholder's place on the continuum:

- **Why**

  Why would we do this? Why does our customer need this? Do they know they need this? How do the industry dynamics, market attractiveness, and competitive landscape make this an appealing proposition for us? Why will we win in the market? What about our core competencies, business model, brand reputation, or strategic position make us likely to win in the marketplace?

  At this point of the continuum, while you do not get into details of what the company will do and how it will do it, you will need to have data to back up your conclusions and hypotheses about why the product is a worthy corporate bet. For example, if you say the market is attractive enough for entry, be ready to substantiate your position with addressable market sizing information.

- **What**

  What are we planning to do to win in the marketplace? What actions will we take? What solutions will we build? What is our approach to customer acquisition? What is our positioning strategy? Will we be able to price the solution competitively?

  At this point, you are getting into more specifics about a potential solution. You are not yet getting into the nitty-gritty details of how it will come about, but you are providing more information on what a viable solution might look like.

- **How**

  How will we build the solution? Will our current platforms work for this? Do we have the talent and capacity to build the envisioned solutions? What technologies will be used? How will we validate, test, and deploy?

Here is where you finally start getting into the minutiae of defining the product, experimenting with various designs, iterating on functionality, and collaborating on the most viable, creative, and valuable final solution.

Executives and cross-functional leaders tend to stay on the left side of the continuum, caring mostly about the whys behind proposed bets and some level of what the company will do about it. They often do not need or want to get into the details of how a solution is going to be built. Everyone on the core product team (product managers, engineers, user experience and design experts, product marketers) needs to understand the varying points of view across the continuum. Others in the product ecosystem will fall at various spots on the continuum, and may even move around, so they need different levels of information at varying times.

Use the message continuum during your preparation for meetings and communications. Consider where on the continuum an audience falls, and then approach your messaging and level of detail accordingly.

CLARITY

What is the point of communicating if our message gets lost and we are constantly clarifying what we meant? The clearer we are in our communication, the more efficient everything around us becomes. Great product managers ensure clarity by being concise and consistent.

Concision

> *As I have said over and over in this book, you must be very concise in how you speak to all of the various audiences you deal with every single day. What I mean by that is various people have different needs from you. Finance needs one thing. Engineering may need something altogether different. Sales needs yet another. I just want you to remember that it is really . . .*

OMG, GET TO THE POINT!

> *Various audiences have different needs and expectations, and you must adjust accordingly.*
> See how easy that was?

Learning how to succinctly communicate is one of the most valuable skills you can ever develop. Concise speech grabs your audience's attention and is more memorable because there is less noise obstructing the message.

Verbosity is often a symptom of nerves. When caught off guard, it is quite natural to become frazzled and drone on in your response. Fear of public speaking is very common, impacting up to 75 percent of the population.[7] Public speaking does not only mean being on a stage in front of thousands of people. Presenting your product strategy to a group of stakeholders is public speaking. Even a one-on-one conversation with a teammate is a form of public speaking. You must convey ideas and connect with others, and that can be nerve-racking.

Each person is at a different place in their journey. If you are already comfortable speaking in front of and with people, you may not need as much advice here. If you are newer to the product manager role or are not yet confident in this skill, the best way to hone it is simply to prepare.

Prepare

Preparation is key to successful communication. The more prepared you are, the more precise your message will be. Below are some tips and methods you can use:

- **Create an Outline or Mind Map**
  To organize your thoughts, create an outline or a mind map of the most important points you want to make and the information needed to augment those points. On your first pass, you may end up with too much and need to pare down. There should only be two to three main points that you are trying to convey. Anything more is too much to absorb in one sitting.
- **Write it Out and Edit**
  Even if you are communicating verbally, it often helps to write a full script of what you plan to say, word for word. Once you have a draft of the script, read it from beginning to end. You will almost certainly find unneeded repetition, filler phrases, or other immaterial details. Edit those out. Shrink the script to only the most important points, eliminating words and phrases that add nothing to the main point.
- **Be Direct**
  Be tactful but say what you mean. Do not sugarcoat it with unnecessary platitudes. Err on the side of simplicity. Even if the subject matter is complex, convey ideas in the simplest, most direct way possible. Construct your communication such that if a person new to the company or the industry were in the meeting, they would understand the gist of your message and would not need you to continuously explain or define what you were saying.

- **Anticipate Questions**

  People tend to drone on when they are caught off guard with a question and are ill-prepared to answer it. Before a meeting or presentation, consider the perspectives of those who will be in the audience. Think about where they fall on the message continuum and what questions they are likely to ask based on their interests. Prepare answers to these questions.

- **Make Presentations Concise and Engaging**

  If you visually present your concepts using PowerPoint, Google Slides, or another method as you speak, follow these rules for concision:

  ○ **Less Is More**

   The slides do not need to include every word you intend to say. Short statements and no more than about six bullet points per slide are best. Avoid the fluff of animations, sound effects, or anything else that does not materially add to the presentation.

  ○ **Use Visuals**

   When possible, use a picture or graph to convey a message. However, avoid anything that requires you to say something like, "I know this is really small, I hope you all can see it." If you have to say that something is too small, leave it out.

- **Practice**

  Any skill we want to perfect takes practice. The more practice you have at speaking, the more prepared and confident you will become and the more adept you will be. One way to do this is by practicing at home. Present to your mirror or to your spouse (or if you are like me, to your cats). Make this a full dress rehearsal and practice the speech or presentation just as you will present it during the actual meeting. Time yourself and then try to cut back if it is too long. Edit to simplify and get to your points quicker. Do not forget to practice answering anticipated audience questions. Time yourself on those as well, and take steps to shorten them if needed.

Of course, you cannot do all this preparation for every single meeting or communication you have with teammates. But absolutely follow some of these tips for the most important meetings, speeches, or presentations. The more you prepare and practice the skills and messages behind these types of meetings, the more confident you will be in the transactional, spontaneous communications you have every day.

Consistency

Some messages are so important that you must consistently repeat them so your teammates absorb and retain them. For example, can you recite your company's vision statement? I mean right now, without having to go look on the website or in your notes to remind yourself. If you are like most people, you cannot.

I am confident that you intrinsically recognize the importance of aligning your product goals with your company's goals, so it makes sense that knowing your company's future direction is important to your success. But even while knowing that, you likely were not able to rattle off your company's vision statement from memory. That is because you probably only hear it once or twice a year at all-hands meetings. Studies have long shown that repetition is one of the most significant variables that impacts memory. Repetition actually stimulates chemical reactions in the brain that help create long-term memory.[8]

Here are some messages that are valuable to consistently repeat, along with examples:

- Your product's vision statement
  - *To make drivers safer and smarter*
- Your product's strategic pillars
  - *Enter the EMEA market by 2024*
  - *By 2023, every product in the portfolio will be a connected device, accessible by the mobile app.*
- How we will win statements
  - *Device users who also download the associated app are 20 percent more satisfied with the product (as indicated via CSAT score). We will win by getting over 90 percent of device users to download the app.*

To ensure everyone in your product ecosystem knows the messages that are most important to success, repeat those messages frequently and consistently. I used to read my product's vision statement aloud at the beginning of every meeting with my teammates. I have also seen teams do this in their daily standups. They literally recited the product vision statement *every single day.* If that is a little too authoritarian, "pledge-your-allegiance-to-the-product" for your taste, find a natural cadence that works for your team. Just be consistent. It will pay off.

KEY TAKEAWAYS

- Great product managers are master communicators.
- Communication in product management is buoyed by two key elements: connection and clarity.
- Storytelling, intentional listening, and adapting to your audience are ways to enhance connections with others.
- Concision and consistency encourage clear messaging.

GREAT PRODUCT MANAGERS HAVE UNCOMMONLY GOOD JUDGMENT

According to *Merriam-Webster's Collegiate Dictionary*, judgment is "the process of forming an opinion or evaluation by discerning and comparing."[9] For many, this truth is an intimidating one to try to build because judgment can feel quite nebulous. People who display good judgment often seem as though they are working off a "gut feeling," but it is really a combination of experience and some key behaviors that leads to better judgment.

Any decision is made through a process that looks something like this: identify the issue and the alternatives at hand, gather pertinent information, make the decision, and then, after an appropriate amount of time, review how the decision worked out. The better judgment a person has, the more efficiently and effectively they can navigate this decision-making process.

Let me be clear: good judgment does not mean always picking the right answer. In fact, in product management, there is rarely a clear "right" and "wrong" answer. We often choose among several good options, and we choose the one we believe is best according to the information we have at the time. But even the very best product manager gets it wrong sometimes. That is just part of the job we all signed up for. What great product managers do is set themselves up for making better decisions through ongoing efforts on two important fronts: they challenge biases when gathering information, and they become comfortable with ambiguity.

CHALLENGING BIASES

Decisions are made through an evaluation of information. Cognitive biases are prevalent in product management and can impact the quality of the information we use for making decisions. Information is gathered continuously, not only transactionally at every decision point, so avoiding biases must be integrated into our ongoing activities.

Some common biases in product management are outlined below.

Solution Bias

Some years ago, my wife and I moved from Chicago to Dallas and were in the process of selling our condo in Chicago. We got an offer, went through the requisite hullabaloo of repair requests from the buyer, and settled on a mutually agreeable price and closing conditions.

We were scheduled to close the transaction on a Friday morning in November. We were already living in Dallas, so the night before the closing, we flew from Dallas to Chicago. After the obligatory Chicago-in-winter flight delays, we landed at O'Hare airport at about 8 p.m. We made our way to the condo to ensure it was ready for the next morning's closing. Our belongings had already been moved out, and the week prior we had hired a cleaning crew so that it was tidy for the new owners. Only a quick once-over was needed before we headed to dinner with some friends and then the hotel for a relaxing evening.

The condo was a typical two-level, "duplex-down," which means that our condo was the unit at the bottom of the building. Our unit's lower level was a semi-basement, so half of it was above ground and half was underground. When we got to the condo, the upper floor looked fine, so we headed down to the lower level. We turned the light on and instantly noticed a large wet spot covering about a third of the carpet.

Panic set in.

Here is my question to you: *What did we need at that moment?*

If you answered, *A wet vacuum! A plumber! Towels! Vodka!* you would have answered it the same way we did. In our minds, we absolutely *needed* all those things—and very quickly (especially the vodka). But a wet vac, a plumber, towels, and even vodka are *solutions*, not needs.

Of course, when you are in that situation, you would never sit down and say, "Okay, we really need to think this through. Let's take the time to dig deep and find our core needs before jumping to any particular solution." Had I said that to my wife, I may very well be divorced right now.

Of course, we jumped into action. After calling the plumber, we found the issue and resolved it (it was actually a small problem with no long-term implications). We rented a wet vac, bought some fans, and went to work, staying up all night to clean up the basement, and we closed on time the following morning.

Back to my question: *What was our real need?* You could say what we really needed was a dry floor. The solutions we chose certainly gave us a dry floor. But I would argue that we had an even more fundamental need: to eliminate the financial burden of owning two homes. *We needed to sell the condo!*

The truth is, another solution to meet that fundamental need would have been to have our real estate agent contact the buyers, tell them the situation, give them assurance the issue was small and taken care of, and offer some monetary credit on the sale for the clean-up effort and hassle. That solution may or may not have worked, but it is a viable solution that we could have explored.

Because we immediately jumped into solution mode, we never explored any other options. We stayed up until 4 a.m. to execute the solution we chose and ultimately met our fundamental need— we sold the condo at 9 a.m. the next day. Had we explored other options, we may have met our need while still getting to enjoy an evening out in Chicago (with some of that vodka).

Product managers are inundated with information and requests. We receive requests from customers, the sales team, bosses, and peers. Inexperienced product managers often move straight into building the requested feature or product—falling prey to solution bias. Great product managers, however, understand that while the term "need" is often used ("We need our products to do so-and-so"), in actuality, customers and internal partners typically speak in solution-specific terms, and more investigation is needed to understand what the core need really is.

Remember, no one needs a wet vac; they need to sell their condo.

Confirmation Bias

> *What the human being is best at doing is interpreting all new information so that their prior conclusions remain intact.*
> —Warren Buffet

Confirmation bias is the tendency to interpret new evidence as confirmation of one's existing beliefs or theories. This is one of the most common biases, and we are all guilty of it.

Confirmation bias examples abound in business and in life. Predispositions are ingrained in each of us based on our unique personal experiences. Eyewitness accounts of crimes, religious beliefs, and political views are often impacted by confirmation bias. Eyewitnesses of a crime are impacted by events in their past. Studies show that religious people see certain events as preordained miracles because they strongly believe in their god. Nonreligious people see the same events as random. All of us are guilty of interpreting information to adhere more closely to our side of the political landscape.

One way confirmation bias often crops up in product management is when we ignore feedback that does not match our current beliefs. Generally, organizations look for patterns; they strive to build once and sell to many. Hearing feedback from one customer does not equate to market demand. Hearing the same thing from multiple customers becomes a pattern. However, we often dismiss the one-off comment as an exception because it is contrary to what we already believe. If a customer tells us that our product idea does not add value or solve a problem for them, we often dismiss that feedback instead of digging deeper to find out whether it has merit and if other customers feel the same.

Business cases are another breeding ground for confirmation bias. Many organizations use business cases as part of their process to investigate the value of a potential large investment. The case should explore a potential investment, presenting the reasons an organization should or should not spend its time, money, and human talent on the opportunity. However, the business case process in most organizations turns out to be nothing more than a search for data that confirms the prevailing belief that a project should move forward. If you use business cases in your organization, think about how many you have been involved with that have ended in a recommendation to not go forward with an opportunity. My guess is that a vast majority of the cases you can think of—and maybe all of them—ended up as a recommendation to move forward. Business cases are usually a second or third step in a linear decision-making process, meaning there has already been at least one decision made that the idea has enough merit to keep investigating. So, we go into the business case process under the assumption that it is a good idea. If confirmation bias was not so prevalent, I believe we would see more of the investigations result in evidence that disproves our assumption.

Framing

One of the most common biases that impacts product managers is framing. Framing refers to the fact that a person reacts differently to information based on how that information is presented.

Consider this example:

Scenario One:
In the United States, only 0.3 percent of the population will die from COVID-19.

Scenario Two:
In the United States, almost one million people will die from COVID-19.

Which scenario sounds better? Scenario one may sound more palatable to you than scenario two. In actuality, the scenarios are the same. The population of the United States is roughly 329.5 million. As of early 2022, about 985,000 people had died from COVID-19 in the United States. That is roughly 0.29 percent of the total population. Both scenarios are the same, but you may have reacted differently based on how each was presented.

Framing is used in sales and marketing quite often. Obviously, we want our product to be perceived in the most positive light possible.

To give you an example, in a television advertisement for a pet food product, two pet owners are shown coming out of a pet store, each with their adorable dog and a bag of dog food in their cart. One woman mentions to the other that the dog food she bought has superior ingredients. The other woman, rightfully shamed for buying the inferior brand for her pup, says, "Yes, but that product is so much more expensive!"

"Oh no!" the first woman exclaims. "I've done the math, and it's only 45 cents more per day."

No excuses now! Only 45 cents a day for sweet Fido to have the best food? Only the most coldhearted pet owner would not choose that, right?

This is a textbook example of framing. 45 cents per day equates to $164.25 over the year. But "45 cents" sounds better than "164 dollars," no? Fido might be just fine with the cheap stuff now that we think about it.

In many cases, there is nothing inherently wrong with framing. It really is only 45 cents more per day to feed Fido the swanky food, so why wouldn't that pet food company try to position its product in the best light? But when product managers solicit feedback from customers, we try not to convince them of anything. In fact, quite the opposite. We do not want to lead them into an answer based on the way we pose the question. So, we must ask questions in such a way that ensures we get unfiltered, unbiased responses.

Sometimes, two of our cognitive biases work together in accordance to sabotage our feedback-gathering even more.

Consider this exchange:

Product Manager (PM) to Customer:	*Our new product detects radiation in the air within a six foot radius, two feet further than our previous product. How does that sound?*
Customer:	*That sounds like a nice improvement.*
PM:	*That's what we were thinking! Thanks so much for your valuable feedback.*
PM, back at the office:	*Woohoo, I knew this would be a great feature! The customer confirmed it.*

Again, the questions we ask and the ways in which we ask them impact the responses we receive. And when we already have a preconceived notion that the product is valuable, we are subconsciously searching for information to confirm that belief. The product manager in this scenario posed the statement in such a way that it had no real relevance to the customer. On the surface, the improvements do sound valuable.

Who would not want to improve radiation detection? The customer gave a generic response to a generic question. The product manager then took that response as confirmation of what he already believed.

Let's look at the same scenario with the question framed differently:

PM to Customer: *How would being able to detect radiation in the air within a six foot radius impact your employees?*

Customer: *Well, we have new policies that require employees to stay at least ten feet away from the reactors, so I don't think that would have much impact.*

PM: *Oh, interesting. Thanks for the feedback.*

In this case, the product manager frames the question in such a way that puts the customer's business and employees into the conversation, making it more relevant. He also allows for more open-ended answers, which leads to more feedback. He learned that while six feet may be an improvement over an older version of the product, it still may not meet a core customer need.

Functional Fixedness

Functional fixedness is a cognitive bias that drives people to use objects only in the traditional ways in which they have seen the object used.

This comes into play with product managers because we are accustomed to the ways in which our products are typically used. It is difficult for us to imagine them being used in varying ways for different problems. As product managers, we must be antennae for the signals of possible new uses for our products. We cannot fall victim to assuming our product is only good for one thing.

Consider the following examples:

- To reduce passenger wait times, a large global elevator company originally designed a buttonless elevator that was controlled by a mobile app. But the COVID-19 pandemic led the company to realize that touch-free surfaces are also quite useful for hygiene and safety.
- Pfizer was looking for a solution to cardiovascular problems when they were researching sildenafil, the active ingredient in what became Viagra. They intended the drug to dilate the heart's blood vessels by blocking a protein called PDE-5. In early clinical trials, however, sildenafil did not seem to help dilate the blood vessels in the heart. But guess what side effect was being reported by men in the clinical trials? And just like that, the little blue pill was born.
- Bubble wrap was originally designed as textured wallpaper. Can you imagine how much fun a bubble wrap house would be at parties? Alas, no one really wanted weird bubbles on their walls, so the inventors eventually offered it to IBM as packing material for their newly built gigantic computer.
- Speaking of odd wallpaper-related product pivots, Play-Doh, the colored children's molding clay, was originally invented in the 1930s as a wallpaper cleaner.
- Arm & Hammer baking soda has been around since 1846 and was originally marketed for cooking and cleaning. In the years since, the product portfolio has blossomed into toothpaste, laundry detergent, and refrigerator and household deodorizer.

We must keep our ears and eyes open to feedback and observations that may lead us to new uses, customer segments, and markets for our products.

BEING COMFORTABLE WITH AMBIGUITY

There are often no clear-cut answers in product management. Rarely are we confronted with a clearly great choice and a clearly awful choice. *Should we do this thing that every single customer has been begging for, or should we do this thing that every customer says is stupid?* Hmm, tough choice. Of course, that does not happen. We are often dealing with various options, all of which could be viable, and we rarely have data that points us to one obvious direction.

There are no sure bets in product management. Virtually everything we do is a prediction about some future outcome. We predict which problem to solve for the customer. We predict which solution will best solve that problem. We predict what the market will look like in three years and what revenue our predicted solution to our predicted problem will reap in that market.

Because of this ambiguity, many product managers fall prey to the tendency to favor the known over the unknown. This is actually another cognitive bias called uncertainty aversion.

There is a proverb that says, "Better the devil you know than the devil you don't," which means it is often better to choose an unwanted or safe option that you are familiar with rather than an option that is unknown to you. This proverb is often used when talking about politics. Many people will vote for the "devil they know"—the politician on whom there is historical data about past votes, stances on issues, or grades from special interest groups. None of this information exists on a new politician, so voters cannot be certain of any future actions. Many would rather err on the side of the known rather than taking a risk on the unknown, even if the known is not a particularly desirable choice.

The same thing happens when product managers choose which ideas they should pursue. Our uncertainty bias often drives us to overinflate the value of a known quantity—a geographic market we have been doing business in, an industry we already sell into, a product type or technology we are comfortable building— and downplay the value of a new market, industry, or technology. We are simply more comfortable with something that provides a bit more certainty.

In the early 1980s, AT&T commissioned McKinsey & Company to estimate the number of mobile phone users there would be in the world by the year 2000. After researching the telecommunications industry and assessing the mobile phone products at the time—heavy, big (remember the "brick phone"?), limited battery, poor network—McKinsey estimated there would be 900,000 mobile phone users in the world by the turn of the century. 900 thousand! In the whole world! To put this into perspective, the actual number of mobile phone users in 2000 ended up being close to 740 million, 822 times more than McKinsey estimated. By 2025, there is projected to be over 8.4 billion mobile phone users in the world.[10]

I was not in the room while the McKinsey consultants were poring over the data, debating among themselves, and ultimately coming up with that ill-fated number (900 thousand!), but I would bet that discomfort surrounding an ambiguous new technology and market drove them to play it safe in their estimates. Even brilliant people, which most of the folks at McKinsey are, can succumb to this. Deferring to the known historic telecommunications industry and the poor reality of the early mobile phone clouded the company's judgment on what could be. Of course, it is easy for us to scoff at that ridiculous forecast now, and none of us may have accurately predicted the utter world-changing impact that mobile phones eventually had. But it is safe to say this is a cautionary tale of how ambiguity can make us uncomfortable, and our predictions and decisions can suffer as a result.

Sorting the Wheat from the Chaff

Living in ambiguity does not necessarily mean having a shortage of data. We are often inundated with all sorts of information and data, but not all of it is material to the problem at hand. There is a saying that is applicable here: "Sort the wheat from the chaff." In agriculture, the chaff is the husk around a seed. In crops such as wheat, the seed is typically what humans eat, so there is a process of removing the chaff to get to the valuable seed. "Sorting the wheat from the chaff" has come to mean being able to distinguish the meaningful from the worthless, which is an exceptionally valuable skill for product managers. Every piece of information is not equal in value. Some information is incredibly pertinent; some is superfluous. Using the right data at the right time is a key skill in good judgment. For example, in the McKinsey cell phone example, the company seemingly relied heavily on data from markets that had an extensive landline infrastructure, estimating the adoption curve of people moving from landline to mobile. But it failed to adequately identify the future trend that countries without landlines would have on cell phone adoption. Instead of building landline infrastructure, many of these countries jumped straight to mobile technology, vastly growing the number of cell phone users worldwide.

Redefining Failure

> *I never lose. I either win or I learn.*
>
> —Nelson Mandela

What do the game of baseball and product management have in common? There is as much failure as there is success, even with the best teams and the best players. The goal of a batter in baseball is to get a hit. A player's batting average is the average number of times he gets a hit when he goes up to bat. A perfect batting average is 1.000 and is called "batting a thousand." No one bats a thousand, at least not over any period of at-bats.

The best career batting average in Major League Baseball history was Ty Cobb's .366, which means he got a hit 36.6 percent of the time he went up to bat. In other words, the best batter in Major League Baseball history, statistically speaking, failed 63.4 percent of the time! Hall of Famer Ted Williams once said that baseball is perhaps the only field in which a person can be successful three out of ten times and be considered a good performer at their job.[11]

While our success is not as easy to measure in product management (we do not always have easy statistics like number of hits divided by number of at-bats), we still work in a world where we fail to meet our original goals quite often. A feature does not resonate with users and has low usage, or a new product does not sway customers to switch from their current solution. Like great baseball players who fail to get a hit 70 percent of the time, product managers often miss the mark with their choices. This reality paralyzes many product managers. Fearful of making the wrong decision, they avoid acting, looking for the perfect data to confirm a direction. Great product managers realize there is no perfect data and act anyway.

Beginner's Mind

In the beginner's mind there are many possibilities, but in the expert's there are few.
—Zen master Shunryu Suzuki

Shoshin is a word from Zen Buddhism meaning "beginner's mind." It refers to having an attitude of openness, eagerness, and lack of preconceptions when studying a subject, even when studying at an advanced level, just as a beginner would.

Having a beginner's mind helps us become more comfortable with ambiguity. Beginners live in constant ambiguity. They are yet to have the knowledge or experience that would lead them to confidence and certainty. One main reason people are uncomfortable with making decisions clouded in uncertainty is because of the potential impact on their reputation if the decision goes awry. Novices have the freedom to be wrong. *They're a newbie, they'll learn.* Having a beginner's mind—even when we are no longer beginners—can be powerful.

Several years ago, I joined a healthcare company as head of product. I had a certain level of healthcare domain knowledge but not as much as most of my coworkers, many of whom had spent their entire careers in the industry. As a leader in the organization, I did not want to appear ill-informed. I was nervous about how my new team, new peers, my boss, and her peers would perceive me and my learning curve. However, I also knew I had a lot of product management knowledge that I was bringing to the organization, which was my major contribution to the team. So I intentionally went into the role with a plan to embrace the ambiguity: Do not be afraid to ask questions. Do not be afraid to make suggestions when warranted. Play the newbie card if needed.

When I joined the company, I did just that; I asked a lot of questions. Questions about healthcare terminology. Questions about customers and why they asked for certain things. Questions about our internal work processes. Questions about why exactly those were our internal processes.

I did not intentionally slow down on the questions, but as it turns out, as I grew in confidence and knowledge, that is exactly what I did. As a leader, I often solicit feedback from my direct reports on how I am doing in my job as their manager and generally as a leader in the business. I genuinely want this feedback from the people who work with me daily because it is tremendously valuable. Truthfully, 99 times out of 100, the answer is something like, "Not that I can think of. I think you're doing a good job!" I get it. It is not easy to give your boss constructive criticism.

But one time, the one out of one hundred, I got a response that, to this day, is one of the best pieces of professional advice I have ever received. It was about a year and half into my tenure, and I was meeting with a woman named Kim for one of our periodic one-on-one meetings. I asked, "Is there anything I can be doing better?" As I braced myself for a watered-down response, she said, "Well, let me tell you."

Uh oh.

"When you first arrived," Kim said,

you asked so many questions. You asked about healthcare topics, which helped you learn but also forced us to talk about complex issues in simpler ways than we were used to. We have all been working together for so long, and sometimes you forget that not everyone knows everything. It was helpful to explain it to someone who did not have our tribal knowledge. We all ended up understanding it better, too.

You asked questions about how we did certain things and why we did them that way. That made us take a step back, look at things differently, and question ourselves on whether it was still the right way to do it. You helped us find new, better ways.

Your questions helped you learn, but they also helped all of us learn.

But you've stopped asking questions. You stopped challenging our assumptions. That has hurt us all. You've grown complacent.

Wow. Well, I did ask for it.

I *had* grown complacent. I thought I knew the answers, so the questions were no longer necessary to ask.

As product managers, the more we think we know, the less likely we are to represent the beginner's mind, and in turn, the more ambiguity can slow us down.

TOOLS TO IMPROVE JUDGMENT

Avoiding biases and becoming comfortable in ambiguity are not innate capabilities; they require awareness, intention, and effort to develop. All of us are prone to biases, and it is completely natural to seek comfort in certainty. Four tools can help us with this:

1. The Hypothesis Canvas Exercise
2. The Hypothesis Debate Exercise
3. The Opportunity Spectrum Exercise
4. A Beginner's Mind Interview

The Hypothesis Canvas

In product management, we work off hypotheses. We hypothesize what problems are most important to attempt to solve. We imagine what creative solution will make customers flock to us. We theorize on how our organization's resources and competencies position us for success. The problem is that we often tailor our actions to prove our hypotheses (a form of confirmation bias). One of the most effective ways you can avoid such bias is to not only search for data to justify and prove your hypothesis but also actively look for information that may disprove it.

To do this, you can use the Hypothesis Canvas Exercise. Start by stating your hypothesis, which may follow one of these three templates:

Problem Statement Hypothesis

A problem statement hypothesis is your assumption that a problem exists. No matter how familiar you are with an industry, a customer base, or the perceived problems for that customer base, it is always a good idea to validate whether the problem exists and is material enough to spend time trying to solve it.

Example:

> *{The issue}* is a problem for *{target customer segment / persona}* because of *{the impact the problem has on them}*.

> *{Unreliable internet service}* is a problem for *{school-aged children in rural areas}* because *{they miss important education and experiences when their school is held virtually during the COVID pandemic.}*

Feature / Functionality Hypothesis

Many of our assumptions are based on the viability of a potential solution to solve a problem. This template lays out how we believe a new feature, functionality, or product will benefit the customer.

Example:

> We assume that *{feature / functionality / product}* will help *{target customer}* because it provides them *{benefit}*.

> We assume that *{a mobile hotspot}* will help *{school-aged children in rural areas}* because it provides them *{reliable internet service so they can join their school classes virtually}*.

Feasibility Hypothesis

Often, before we even investigate the feasibility, we assume that our company is capable or incapable of solving a problem based on our expertise, resources, past experiences, or other variables. Assumptions about our abilities are typically rooted in overzealous positivity (*Anything is possible, woohoo!*) or a tenured pessimism (*We have tried that several times over the years and it never works*).

Example:

> We believe we will be able to build {*feature / functionality / product*} because {*ability / resources / experience*}.
>
> We believe we will be able to build {*mobile hotspots*} because {*we have experience in building internet networks*}.

Or

> We believe we will NOT be able to build {*feature / functionality / product*} because {*lack of ability / resources / experience / other hurdles*}.
>
> We believe we will NOT be able to build {*mobile hotspots*} because {*we only have experience building internet networks in urban areas where infrastructure already exists*}.

As you have conversations with customers and go through your market research, actively document the information that may prove your hypothesis *and* the information that may disprove it.

Here is how the exercise might look using the examples above:

Unreliable internet service is a problem for *school-aged children in rural areas* because *they miss important education and experiences when their school is held virtually during the COVID pandemic.*

We assume that *a mobile hotspot* will help *school-aged children in rural areas* because it provides them *reliable internet service so they can join their school classes virtually.*

During your research, you found the following data points:

- **Proving feedback:**
  Almost 30 percent of rural residents in the United States have no broadband internet service at home.[12]
- **Disproving feedback:**
  - Nearly 42 percent of rural schools in the United States continue to offer fully in-person instruction (as compared to 17 percent of urban schools),[13] so not as many rural students may need internet service at home.
  - Three school superintendents in rural school districts all stated that virtual school will not be offered in the next school year regardless of the status of COVID-19.

We believe we will be able to build *mobile hotspots* because *we have experience in building out internet networks.*

- **Proving feedback:**
  We have been in business for 30 years and have provided over 300 communities with internet services.
- **Disproving feedback:**
  Mobile hotspots rely on cellular networks, and we have only two partnerships with cellular networks that have coverage in most major rural areas of the United States.

In this example, we start to lose steam as early as the problem hypothesis stage. The research shows that in-person instruction at rural schools returned at a much higher rate than in urban areas, and conversations with school superintendents in rural areas indicate virtual school will not be happening much longer. Therefore, the benefit of a potential mobile hotspot wanes. The problem is essentially being solved through a return to in-person classes. In this case, even if the team could prove the merits of their abilities to build mobile hotspots, the efforts would likely be for naught. This team should turn its attention elsewhere.

HYPOTHESIS CANVAS

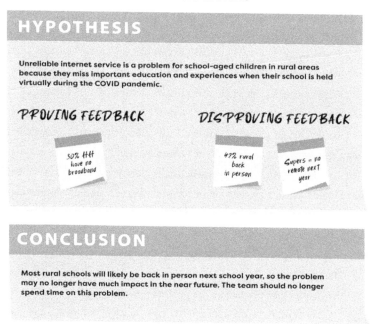

HYPOTHESIS

Unreliable internet service is a problem for school-aged children in rural areas because they miss important education and experiences when their school is held virtually during the COVID pandemic.

PROVING FEEDBACK

30% ††† have no broadband

DISPROVING FEEDBACK

42% rural back in person

Supers = no remote next year

CONCLUSION

Most rural schools will likely be back in person next school year, so the problem may no longer have much impact in the near future. The team should no longer spend time on this problem.

Hypothesis Debate Exercise

Occasionally, you will come to valid conclusions simply by using the Hypothesis Canvas Exercise. There is no real need to go through a debate exercise on the mobile hotspot idea because it has already been determined not to be a particularly viable option.

When a conclusion is still uncertain after your hypothesis canvas work, however, move on to the Hypothesis Debate Exercise. If you ever took a debate class in school, you know how powerful it can be to debate multiple sides of an issue. Think of the hypothesis canvas work as data-gathering to support your debate. The Hypothesis Debate Exercise enables teammates to dive deep into conversation and analysis about the ways in which something could succeed or fail, which opens their minds to all possibilities. This exercise is particularly helpful for combating confirmation bias, functional fixedness, and solution bias.

To conduct this exercise, get a cross-functional group of teammates together—in-person, if possible, but it certainly works virtually as well.

Assign people to three teams: 1) Prove It! 2) Disprove It! 3) Judges.

The Prove It! team is focused on using data and research to argue for the assumption. The Disprove It! team is focused on arguing against the assumption using data that they believe disproves the belief. If someone on the team has a particularly strong opinion for or against an assumption, assign them to the opposite team. It will force them to look at the situation from a different perspective and ensure there is no unintended partiality in the presentation of one side.

The Judges team is the impartial group that will judge the quality of evidence presented by the teams. In the best-case scenario, Judges are peers to the folks on the debate teams. If the Judges are bosses who have decision-making authority, the debate often devolves into an approval exercise. So, choose those who have enough background to understand the domain of the hypotheses being debated but are not partial either way. If finding Judges that fit this mold is not possible, you can complete the exercise without the Judge team as long as all teammates agree to consider all evidence in good faith.

The outcome of the Hypothesis Debate Exercise is a team decision on how to move forward: 1) continue work under the guise that the hypothesis is valid, or 2) scrap it and move on to something else. Remember, the evidence on either side is rarely going to create an ironclad argument. However, one benefit of the exercise is to help the team become more comfortable assessing information so that they can choose a direction even when there is some uncertainty of the eventual outcome.

HYPOTHESIS DEBATE EXERCISE

HYPOTHESIS DEBATE EXERCISE	Prove it! Team:	Disprove it! Team:	Judges:
Product/Opportunity: Date:			

HYPOTHESIS	JUSTIFICATION	COUNTER ARGUMENT
Describe the hypothesis/assumption.	Describe the justification. Use the proving feedback to back your argument.	Describe the counter to the hypothesis and/assumption and the justification for it. Use the disproving feedback to back your argument.

HYPOTHESIS	JUSTIFICATION	COUNTER ARGUMENT

Opportunity Spectrum Exercise

We naturally tend to identify opportunities that fit neatly into our comfort zones. The Opportunity Spectrum Exercise forces the team to explore solutions that run the gamut of perspectives, from safe to uncertain.

First, have the team outline the situation, problem statement, and impacted customer groups. After this context is clear, ask them to brainstorm ideas about how to solve the problem from various standpoints, creating as many ideas as they can think of for each in the allotted time. (About ten to 15 minutes per perspective is usually good but take as long as you need to have the appropriate dialogues.) As you go through this exercise, try to force the team to think of different ideas for each perspective. For instance, it may seem like the same idea could be both the risky solution and the disruptive solution. Spend time ideating separate opportunities for each.

- **The Risky Solution**
  This is a solution involving the most audacious idea the team can think of to solve the problem. It is likely way out of the comfort zone of the organization—one of those ideas about which everyone in the room says, "Yeah right, we'll *really* do that." *eyeroll* Risky solutions are big and bold. High risk, high reward.
- **The Pragmatic Solution**
  This solution is based on an idea that fits squarely into what your organization usually does. No one would bat an eye at this suggestion. It probably does

not inspire any passion, but it does not scare anyone either.

- **The Creative Solution**
  This solution involves an imaginative idea formed by using all the creative juices the team has.

- **The Uninspired Solution**
  An uninspired solution is one based on an idea that most mirrors a competitive offering or is just a different version of something already in your product portfolio.

- **The Disruptive Solution**
  A disruptive solution is an idea that would turn the industry upside down. If your company did this, it would likely be catastrophic to competitors. It would take the world by storm and completely change customer expectations.

- **The Incremental Solution**
  This solution is one that builds on some product, asset, or capability that already exists in the company. It would add value and be an improvement on the status quo but is not going to completely disrupt the product line or the market.

Opportunity Spectrum Exercise

Complete the following summaries for the situation.

SITUATION SUMMARY

PROBLEM STATEMENT	CUSTOMERS/TARGETS IMPACTED

Opportunity Spectrum Exercise

As a team, brainstorm ideas for each perspective. After thinking of several
ideas for each, pick the idea the team believes best represents that perspective.
Then complete the information on the next page.

PERSPECTIVE	IDEAS
the risky solution	
the pragmatic solution	
the creative solution	
the uninspired solution	
the disruptive solution	
the incremental solution	

Opportunity Spectrum Exercise

First, pick ONE idea from each perspective… the one that the team believes best represents that
perspective or has the biggest chance of success. Then discuss the best and worst thing about each
idea. For example: It would be a completely new offering in the market (BEST); It would take us years
of time and loads of money to create (WORST).

PERSPECTIVE	IDEA	BEST THING ABOUT THIS IDEA	WORST THING ABOUT THIS IDEA
the risky solution			
the pragmatic solution			
the creative solution			
the uninspired solution			
the disruptive solution			
the incremental solution			

Opportunity Spectrum Exercise

Are there aspects from various perspective that are attractive? After looking at all perspectives, is there a "hybrid idea" that encompasses parts of multiple ideas the team identified? Pick the top idea (original or hybrid) and other ideas that may be worth investigating further.

From here, have the team go through the list of ideas for each perspective and pick the one idea that they believe best represents that perspective. You will have six ideas at this point: one each for risky, pragmatic, creative, uninspired, disruptive, and incremental. Next, prompt the team to outline what they believe are the best and worst parts of each of those six ideas.

After the team has fully explored the best and worst of the chosen ideas from each perspective, discuss the attractive aspects from all the ideas. Perhaps there was a hybrid idea that encompasses parts of ideas from multiple perspectives. Maybe the risky idea will never fly, but there are some aspects of it you could combine with more realistic ideas to make a substantially valuable offering.

The desired outcome of this exercise is not necessarily to walk away with an idea or two to keep exploring, although that certainly may happen. The real benefit is getting the team thinking in a broader perspective.

Beginner's Mind Interview

In a Beginner's Mind interview with a customer, you ask questions to which you think you already know the answers. It also helps to interview multiple people within the same customer organization. For example, if your customer is a large, big-box retailer, interview the buyer for your product category as well as a store manager. Ask the same questions of both. You will likely get different perspectives from each. You may think you know everything there is to know about the customer, but these interviews invariably bring insights that you had not thought of before.

For this exercise, choose a customer you know fairly well, perhaps one with whom you have conducted other "voice of customer" research.

1. Schedule 30 to 60 minutes with each person you are interviewing. You can conduct the interviews in-person or virtually. I recommend recording the session if your customer agrees. This will help you review the responses and find even more nuance in them than from just memory or notes.
2. At the beginning of the interview, explain to the person that the questions may seem basic but that is intentional. The purpose of the discussion is to look at things from different perspectives, not to test them on their knowledge.

Encourage them to answer the questions to the best of their knowledge and experience.

3. Example questions:
    a. How would you describe {*Company Name*}'s business to someone who has never heard of it?
    b. How does the business make money?
    c. Who are your customers?
    d. What problem(s) are you solving for your customers?
    e. Who are your customers' customers? {*If their customers are not the end-customer*}
    f. What problems do your customers solve for their customers?
    g. Why do your customers choose to do business with you?

This interview may be more difficult than it sounds because we naturally want to sound intelligent and well-versed in all matters, especially when speaking with customers. To practice, start with coworkers and ask them about your own business. You may be surprised at the various perspectives from people and how some of their answers will make you see things slightly differently. Interview a coworker with whom you do not necessarily work with directly every day—perhaps someone in the finance or customer service department who has an ancillary role to yours.

KEY TAKEAWAYS

- Great product managers demonstrate uncommonly good judgment: the process of forming an opinion or evaluation by discerning and comparing.
- Judgment often naturally improves over time with experience but is also anchored in avoiding biases in our work and becoming comfortable with ambiguity.
- Some common cognitive biases in product management are solution bias, confirmation bias, framing, and functional fixedness.
- Ambiguity is a part of product management. There are rarely clear-cut right and wrong answers in the industry. Great product managers learn to find meaningful knowledge in a sea of information, redefine failure to embrace the learning that comes from every experience, and try to apply a beginner's mind.
- Techniques to help build good judgment include the Hypothesis Canvas Exercise, Hypothesis Debate Exercise, Opportunity Spectrum Exercise, and Beginner's Mind Interview.

GREAT PRODUCT MANAGERS ARE FANATICAL ABOUT PRIORITIZING THEIR TIME

Great product managers are fanatical about doing the things that will make the biggest impact on their product. If something does not have a direct or indirect effect on the product, then it is not important enough to do. Prioritizing the work that makes the most impact on customers and our business is one of the most pressing challenges for every product manager. But many product managers are so focused on prioritizing the work—which problems to solve or which features get in a particular release—that they forget prioritization starts with how they use their time. Time is finite. We get the time we have and no more. Truth be told, we do not necessarily need *more* time; we need to better use the time we have. One of the most common mistakes I see product managers make is not prioritizing their own time.

How many Friday afternoons have you looked back on your week and said to yourself, "Well, that week got away from me. All those fire drills and not a single thing checked off my prioritized to-do list"? Great product managers are comfortable letting some fires burn. If something is not their explicit responsibility or it does not have a direct impact on the product, they know that it should not usurp the higher priority tasks. This is one of the hardest lessons product managers must learn. It is not our job to put out every fire or perform all tasks having to do with our product.

A PRODUCT MANAGER'S TIME

Product managers are responsible for researching and uncovering customer problems and then collaborating with internal teammates to design, develop, launch, and support a viable solution that solves that problem and adds value for the customer. It is that simple. And that complicated.

A lot goes into "researching and uncovering customer problems," and even more goes into "collaborating with internal teammates to design, develop, launch, and support a viable solution that solves that problem and adds value for the customer." Product managers are often asked to do more than what should really be part of a product manager's role, frankly. The main reason for this is the organization's lack of understanding about what the product manager role should and should not be. Product management involves many people engaged in numerous processes, activities, workstreams, and decisions, and the lines of responsibility among all those people are often drawn in pencil when they should be in thick black marker. This typically leads to the product manager becoming the catch-all; they are thrown all requests or tasks that are not concretely understood by the organization as belonging to others.

This customer has an urgent question. Send it to Mikey the Product Manager, he will know.

Anybody know when the components are coming in for the product? Call Mikey the Product Manager, he should be able to tell you.

What Mikey said to these requests when he was a new product manager was, "I'll call the customer right now and talk to them about it" and "Let me check with the supply chain managers and get back to you."

What Mikey says now that he is a great, experienced product manager is, "That's a request for the customer support department. They are well-equipped to answer the customer's question. If they ever need me for more guidance, they know to reach out" and "I haven't heard the latest from supply chain managers. Reach out to them since they're the experts."

There are a few areas outside the role where I see product managers spending an inordinate amount of time. Let's talk about what a product manager *is not*.

A Product Manager is Not an Engineer

Many organizations, especially those heavily in science-, technology-, or engineering-based industries, think of product management as an offshoot of engineering. In these organizations, people often internally transition into the product manager position from an engineering role, and product management frequently reports up through the engineering department. When others in the company see this organizational structure or the common engineer-to-product-manager career path, they naturally assume that the product role is an extension of engineering. That then becomes part of the unspoken (mis)understanding of what the product manager job is.

If your company's products are technical-, scientific-, or engineer-driven, it makes sense that the product managers may have a background rooted in science. There is no question that an understanding of the technical details of a product can be an asset to a product manager. But this knowledge cannot be in lieu of a deep understanding of the business side of the product or of customers and their needs. Whether you have an engineering background or not, when you are a product manager, your job is no longer to be an engineer.

A Product Manager is Not Sales Support

A sales engineer role (sometimes called a solutions engineer or presales consultant) is a common sales support job in many industrial and technical companies and is a position designed to be a hybrid of an engineer and a salesperson. This is someone who understands the inner workings of the product but is also adept at translating technical details into language that addresses the customer problem. They can help customers and prospects understand how the product meets their needs. These customers also often need some technical specifications and details to make buying decisions, so the sales engineer is the person who can toggle between the intricacies of technical jargon and the lofty pledges of marketing speak.

Some companies subconsciously deem the product manager as a pseudo sales engineer. They often expect product managers to be subject matter experts during all important sales meetings. While this is sometimes needed in the cases of large customer tenders, when the product manager is engaged in sales calls too often, it takes away from their other responsibilities.

A Product Manager is Not a Data Analyst

Product analytics is becoming more popular and important than ever. Product managers must be comfortable with and adept at using data to understand what is going on with the product and the business and use those insights to make decisions. However, a product manager should not be the person responsible for capturing, sorting, and compiling the data into detailed reports and visualizations. Ideally, the data and reports will be created by someone else in the organization to be utilized by product managers and others.

This was a real issue for one of my customers, a global manufacturer of personal and environmental protective products. The business had multiple manufacturing sites throughout the world, and each of these sites had its own enterprise resource planning system to manage capacity planning, production, budgeting, inventory management, sales information, and accounting. Some product lines were produced at only one manufacturing site with only one system, which made it easier to access and analyze the data on products. But many of the products were built in multiple locations, and product managers would spend two to three full days a month gathering data from the various systems; piecing the data together into a spreadsheet; creating macros, graphs, and tables; and trying to paint a picture of their product's progress. Two to three days per month! That is over ten percent of a product manager's time spent just being a data analyst.

While overhauling the organization's enterprise software infrastructure or enduring a multi-year master data management project certainly may have been valuable in the long-term, those decisions typically resided outside of product management. Needing a solution more quickly, the head of product management hired a couple of product data analysts whose sole responsibility was to create product dashboards and reports for product managers. This gave product managers what they needed to analyze their product's business without having to spend the time creating the reports themselves. The product managers could then spend those two to three days per month working on more strategic tasks.

A Product Manager is Not a Supply Chain Manager or a Capacity Planner

Product managers who work in a manufacturing environment often spend a massive amount of time chasing down information on inventory, parts, and demand forecasts to help steer optimal capacity planning and supply chain management. There are typically talented people in supply chain management and capacity planning roles, but product managers still tend to be the catch-all for questions on these areas. Like Mikey the product manager, colleagues should be encouraged to go directly to the experts with their questions.

A Product Manager is Not Customer Support

Especially in business-to-business (B2B) organizations, the product manager gets pulled into a customer support role quite often. We know the product best, or so it feels to many of our peers, so they naturally ask us to help when a customer is in need. But there should be a dedicated person or group whose sole responsibility is to support the customer with their questions and issues. If the issue rises to the level of urgency, the product manager may certainly get involved to help, but that should be the exception, not the rule.

Let me be clear: There are times when product managers do and should perform the above roles in some capacity. They may think like a problem-solving engineer during a design exercise, serve as a product subject matter expert in an important sales meeting with a customer, or provide support to the warehouse to ensure inventory is kept at an optimal level. But it is important for the organization to understand that the other roles—engineer, sales support, capacity planning—are ultimately responsible for these functions, even when the product manager is involved from time to time. When these types of tasks take up most of a product manager's time, it is time to clarify roles.

MANAGING YOUR TIME FOR WHAT MATTERS

Before you can start prioritizing your time at work, you need to define what is important to you across your whole life. I am not a big believer in looking at a work-life balance in its traditional sense. I think we have evolved from the neatly bifurcated world of "work" and "life." We now have constant access to work through technology, often work remotely from anywhere we want, and communicate at varying times with teammates across time zones. Many of us no longer have a true nine to five job. This can be both good and bad. It means we can attend our child's soccer game on a Wednesday afternoon or take a yoga class on a Tuesday morning and do work at other times. But it also means we run the risk of never being truly "off work," checking our email or other communication channels throughout the day and night.

In the work environments of most product management folks, the world will never return to a clock-in and clock-out environment. So, it has become even more critical for well-being to manage this blending of activities.

The lines between what constitutes professional and personal have blurred. When I exercise, it is obviously not a work task, but it sure does help my energy level when I am working. When I learn something new from a work colleague and feel invigorated and passionate, you bet I still feel happy and motivated—even when I am just at home watching television with my wife and kids (a.k.a. cats). Our lives can energize or fatigue us, and there is little separating those emotions from the job. Similarly, our jobs can empower us or burn us out, and that absolutely impacts the other aspects of our lives.

So, instead of trying to magically balance professional and personal activities on an unrealistic fulcrum, we should harmoniously blend our activities in a way that ultimately creates prolonged contentment. I call this our "contentment mix," the mix of activities that help us feel satisfied, happy, fulfilled, healthy, and productive. Those activities will be both professional and personal. Start by delineating the big buckets of things that make you happiest and most productive. Yes, I realize you may only want to have "Eat doughnuts" and "Lay on a beach" for your perfect contentment mix, but let's be realistic here. What are the things that you must do and the things that you want to do? It might look something like this:

CONTENTMENT MIX

You do not want to get too granular here. Just identify the major things on which you want to spend time, with some relative distribution across all the areas. Everyone's contentment mix is different. Maybe travel is one of your contentment items. Or volunteer work. Mine, of course, would make time for naps and watching *The Golden Girls*. Make your contentment mix personal to what matters to you.

Once you have your full life laid out, you can start breaking down the specifics of the work area of your mix. Remember, you do not necessarily need more time at work; rather, you need to better optimize the time you have. Are you spending your time on the things that will have the most impact on your product and on you as a product manager?

First, deconstruct and evaluate how you currently spend your time by assigning categories to your activities. You can use the VITAL time management tool to help with this. This tool allows you to see where your time is going. Review every work activity you did over the past week or two. If you have the information on everything you did in the past month, that is even better. Make sure to capture every meeting, task, time spent emailing, or any other major workstream that took your time. Go through each activity and map it on the VITAL map.

The categories of a VITAL map are Vital, Important, Transactional, Ancillary, and Learning, and each represents an area where most of your efforts should be going.

- **Vital**
  Vital activities are those that are essential to your product and the core of your product manager role. While you may do it in collaboration with your teammates, you should be the one responsible for these tasks because they directly involve activities or decisions about your product. Examples include voice of customer sessions, design sprints, product strategy generation, and stakeholder meetings.

- **Important**
  Important activities are those that affect your product but are possibly owned by teammates. You should be involved with but not drive these activities. Examples include marketing campaigns for your product, sales demos, engineering reviews, technology architectural decisions, and supply chain updates.

- **Transactional**
  Much of our workday involves simply providing or requesting information or support. These "transactions" often do not themselves have a material impact on the product, but they are an important part of working with others and ensuring work in progress

continues smoothly. These back-and-forth interactions take up more of your time than you may realize. Examples include sending emails to clarify a request, communicating with the team on message apps, and attending meetings to represent the product.

- **Ancillary**

  Ancillary activities support your product but are not led by product managers. You may participate occasionally, but for the most part, these are left to someone else's expertise. Examples include company supplier decisions, distributor discussions, and large business customer relationship meetings.

- **Learning**

  Learning activities are those that help you grow your knowledge about product management, business, your industry, or any other areas of importance to you. Product managers are on a continuous learning journey, so carving out time for learning activities is important. I also include down-time and stress-management activities such as a midday walk or meditation in this category.

VITAL TIME MANAGEMENT EXAMPLE

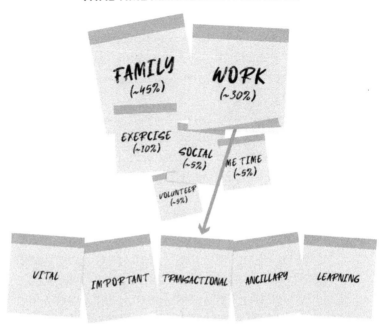

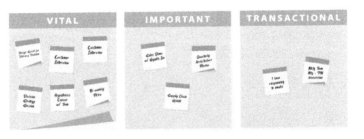

- **Unrelated**

  You may also want to track activities that are unrelated to your product. These are activities that we undertake as employees but are not directly related to our product role. Examples include company-wide meetings, employee resource group participation, and company-wide volunteer hours. While such activities may not take up much of your time, they may be worth noting.

An easy way to use the VITAL model is to color code your calendar to visualize what your upcoming weeks look like in terms of priority. Assign each V-I-T-A-L a different color. When you add a meeting or an activity to your calendar, color code it according to its category. Then look at your calendar. Are too many activities falling into the transactional or ancillary categories? You may want to reprioritize. Are you saving enough time for learning? If not, perhaps reschedule a non-urgent meeting for a few weeks out.

PRIORITIZING FOR YOUR PRODUCT

Of course, it is not enough to optimize only your time; you must also optimize the work that is done on your product. Organizations use many valuable models to prioritize their product work. Some of the most popular include the following:

- Vision versus Survival—part of the Radical Product Thinking approach by Radhika Dutt, this two-by-two matrix helps visualize the tradeoffs between making progress toward your long-term vision (vision fit) and mitigating short-term risk (survival)[14]

- Kano—prioritizes features based on the likelihood that they will satisfy customers
- MoSCoW—places work into four categories: must have, should have, could have, and won't have
- Cost of Delay—represents the economic impact of delaying a project or piece of work
- RICE—scores items on four factors: reach, impact, confidence, and effort

I am not going to tell you which model is best for your team—although I will say that I particularly appreciate Radhika Dutt's vision versus survival approach because when short-term decisions are needed for valid reasons, this model at least brings transparency and acknowledgement of some future debt we may have to pay.

Truthfully, all prioritization methods have pros and cons. Regardless of which works best for your organization, before implementing any framework, your team must collectively agree on a few things:

- **Identify the Team's Comfort Level with Subjectivity.**
  Some teams are skeptical of anything less than empirical, quantitative proof. Others rely on data plus gut and accept a level of subjectivity. When determining which framework will work best for your team, pay attention to the type of data (qualitative, more subjective versus quantitative, less subjective) each framework calls for, and judge accordingly.
- **Commit to Holding Each Other Accountable for Validating Data.**
  Even with some of the less subjective inputs, validation is important. Teams must challenge each other—in healthy, productive ways—when inputs are

introduced without the proper validation. If someone suggests an item is of "high value" to the customers, ask which customers have validated that assumption. If someone says a feature is "high effort," talk to them about why that is so and whether there are other ways to think about the effort it would take. Not everything needs to become a contrarian debate, but do not default to taking everything at face value. Any prioritization effort is only as good as the input going into it, so ensure you have validated your assumptions.

- **Agree Ahead of Time on How Disputes Will Be Handled.**

  What criteria will be used to break ties? Does anyone have veto power? Who will make the final decision if the team is at an impasse? These are important questions to answer ahead of time.

Whether you pick one of the models listed above, implement another one, make up your own, or choose none at all, make sure you are always asking and answering the following three questions on any proposed effort for the team. At the end of the day, a vast majority of prioritization can be accomplished through understanding these three things:

1) **Does it matter to customers?**

   You may also need to answer sub questions:

   a. **If so, how many customers? Is it important to one big customer or a larger swath of the customer base?**

      This is important to know because we generally do not want to build something simply because one customer requested it.

   b. **Which customers?** (target segments, persona, or another category)

This can be important because some segments may be more important or strategic for the organization than others.

If you cannot answer the first question in the affirmative, why are you even considering it? You should probably just move on to something else. If you answer yes to question one, move on to question two:

2) **Will customers pay for it?**
   A potential sub question with related considerations may also need to be asked:

   If not, is there residual value to other offerings? Does it shore up a portfolio gap that then allows for increased sales? Does it contribute to customer retention even if it does not produce incremental new revenue?

If you can answer question two or its sub questions affirmatively, move on to question three:

3) **Is it taking you in a direction you want to go?**
   Also consider some potential sub questions:
   a. **Is it where you want your product to go?**
   b. **Is it where your company wants to go?**

Even if you answer yes to questions one and two, that does not necessarily mean the product is aligned with your organization or product strategy. Question three asks you to examine the long-term impact of the product. For example, if it is something that could sell quite well but requires you to focus on a geographic market or industry that you intend to exit or deprioritize over the next few years, you will need to decide what is best. Sometimes the few years of additional income from a legacy market allows us some leeway for focusing on a few riskier but higher-growth efforts. Other times, it simply drains resources that could be used in more strategic areas. Therein lies the importance of your judgment. No prioritization matrix can replace your experience and judgment.

KEY TAKEAWAYS

- Great product managers are fanatical about prioritizing their time and effort.
- Product managers are often asked to take on too many tasks that belong under other roles: engineer, data analyst, sales support, operations, and customer service.
- Establish a contentment mix to align what really matters to you across your life.
- Use the VITAL tool to determine where your time at work is being spent: vital, important, transactional, ancillary, or learning tasks.
- When prioritizing the work the product team does, always answer these three questions, regardless of what prioritization framework you choose to use:
  1. Does it matter to customers?
  2. Will customers pay for it?
  3. Is it taking you in a direction you want to go?

THE COHESION OF
THE FIVE TRUTHS

People have asked me which of the immutable truths is most important. The fact is, I do not see them as individual truths as much as an interconnected foundation that makes navigating the world of product management easier. The truths do not exist in silos; they interact and impact each other continuously. After a while, we do not even realize the truths are driving our behaviors.

Here are some of the ways I have seen the truths work together to make a positive impact in product teams:

- When things start going astray on a project, a release, or just in general working conditions, quick and straightforward communication can get things back on track. The longer we let things simmer, the worse they will get. Strong relationships and good communication can nip this in the bud and get us going again.

- A deep understanding of the customer leads to better prioritization. If we know what will make a difference with the customer, it is much easier to place those things at the top of our list. Accurate prioritization of product work is virtually impossible without a high level of customer intelligence.

- Good relationships make work more fun, and it is hard to overstate the importance of an enjoyable environment. We may not love every moment of every day, but I have yet to see a team be consistently successful in a toxic environment.

- The more product managers demonstrate good judgment, the more credibility they will have with teammates. The more confidence the team has in them, the better the relationships become. The better the relationships are, the better the team will work together.

- When a product manager is good at communicating the story of "why" behind the team's actions, everyone around understands the bigger picture and can carry that through their work. Product managers who talk about the "how" too much will not be as effective as when they consistently share the story of the "why." This key communication skill leads to team cohesion through shared purpose.

- Judgment is enhanced by knowledge, of course, but it is also enhanced by self-confidence. Few things make someone question their own judgment more than a lack of confidence in their knowledge and ability. When product managers know they have done the work to understand the customer and uncover the customer's needs, they are more apt to feel comfortable making recommendations and decisions. Confident people communicate better. They build healthier relationships. They prioritize more effectively. And they learn from their mistakes and move on without losing confidence in their overall ability. If there is one thing that the five truths give more than anything else, it is confidence. And that confidence impacts practically everything a product manager does.

CONCLUSION:
MAKING THESE
YOUR TRUTHS

As I have said before, building your immutable truths should not be an insurmountable task. Anyone can build these capabilities if they put the time, effort, and diligence into it. The time you put into this now will pay dividends in the future and be one of the most important investments you will ever make in your career.

The best way to be intentional about your efforts is to make and follow a plan. You can use the template below to sketch out the ways in which you want to approach this and measure yourself along the way.

MY IMMUTABLE TRUTHS Progress Plan/ Monthly Journal	TRUTH:	MONTH:
LEARNINGS What did you learn about this Truth ?	**ACTIONS** What did you do to improve this skill ?	
MISSTEPS Did you make any mistakes from which you can learn ?	**MOST EXCITING** What most excites you about what your learned or did this month on this Truth ?	
NEXT STEPS What can you do from here to keep improving this your skills on this Truth ?		

My recommendation is to assess where you stand today on each of the truths. From there, create a development plan prioritizing where you believe you are weakest. For example, if your relationships are the thing holding you back the most, start there. Use some of the tools in the book to start assessing and building better relationships. If communication seems to be your weakness, try to improve in that area first. And so on.

Rate Yourself on the IMMUTABLE Truths

1 = I am new to this and have no skills yet
2 = I have only a little experience with this
3 = I have some skills but lots of room for improvement
4 = I am not quite an expert but am very good at this truth
5 = I feel I am an expert on this

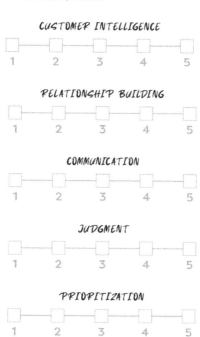

CUSTOMER INTELLIGENCE

1   2   3   4   5

RELATIONSHIP BUILDING

1   2   3   4   5

COMMUNICATION

1   2   3   4   5

JUDGMENT

1   2   3   4   5

PRIORITIZATION

1   2   3   4   5

Finally, give yourself time, space, and understanding. Do not be too hard on yourself if you have some missteps or occasionally do not seem to be moving the needle on these skills. You will become great at them, but it will take time, and you never really stop learning and improving. There will be a time when it just clicks, and you feel you have made real progress. There will also be times when you feel you have not improved at all. Remember that every task, every interaction, every release, everything you do in product management can be used as a learning experience and a stepping stone to better skills. So, even if you sometimes feel as though you are not giving your development plan enough focus, you are surreptitiously constructing a better you with every new experience.

This is a journey. Be kind to yourself along the way.

ENDNOTES

1. "Our Path to an All-Electric Future," General Motors, accessed February 16, 2022, https://www.gm.com/electric-vehicles.
2. Jonathan Trout, "The 5 Whys Method: Getting to the Root Cause Quickly," ReliablePlant, accessed March 8, 2022, https://www.reliableplant.com/5-whys-31870.
3. ThinkReliability, "Toyota Welding Robot 5-Why," accessed February 16, 2022, https://www.thinkreliability.com/toyota-welding-robot-5-why/.
4. Wanis H. Ibrahim, "Recent Advances and Controversies in Adult Cardiopulmonary Resuscitation," Postgraduate Medical Journal 83, no. 984 (October 2007): 649–654, http://dx.doi.org/10.1136/pgmj.2007.057133.
5. Adam M. Grant, *Think Again: The Power of Knowing What You Don't Know* (New York: Viking Books, 2021).
6. Brennan White, "A Guide to Storytelling Possibilities," Cortex Automation Inc., December 6, 2018, https://www.meetcortex.com/blog/why-we-empathize-with-characters.
7. Rosemary Black, "Glossophobia (Fear of Public Speaking): Are You Glossophobic?" Psycom, last modified September 12, 2019, https://www.psycom.net/glossophobia-fear-of-public-speaking#:~:text=Glossophobia%2C%20or%20a%20fear%20of,full%2Don%20panic%20and%20fear.
8. Gretchen Schmelzer, "Understanding Learning and Memory: The Neuroscience of Repetition," January 11, 2015, http://gretchenschmelzer.com/blog-1/2015/1/11/understanding-learning-and-memory-the-neuroscience-of-repetition.
9. *Merriam-Webster's Online Collegiate Dictionary*, 11th ed., s.v. "Judgment," accessed March 7, 2022, https://www.merriam-webster.com/dictionary/judgment.
10. "Mobile Phone Market Forecast—2019," International Telecommunication Union, last updated January 23, 2019, https://stats.areppim.com/stats/stats_mobilex2019.htm.

11. "Ted Williams Quotes," Baseball Almanac, accessed February 20, 2022, https://www.baseball-almanac.com/quotes/quowilt.shtml.

12. Emily A. Vogels, "Some Digital Divides Persist Between Rural, Urban and Suburban America," Pew Research Center, August 19, 2021, https://www.pewresearch.org/fact-tank/2021/08/19/some-digital-divides-persist-between-rural-urban-and-suburban-america/.

13. Heather L. Schwartz, Melissa Kay Diliberti, Lisa Berdie, David Grant, Gerald P. Hunter, and Claude Messan Setodji, "Urban and Rural Districts Showed a Strong Divide During the COVID-19 Pandemic," Rand Corporation 2021 Research Report, accessed February 20, 2022, https://www.rand.org/pubs/research_reports/RRA956-2.html.

14. Dutt, R., *Radical Product Thinking* (Berrett-Koehler Publishers 2021).

ABOUT THE AUTHOR

JJ Rorie is an advisor, coach, speaker, and teacher, specializing in a practical, relatable, and enjoyable approach to learning the product management craft. Through her work with thousands of product managers, she pioneered the *5 Immutable Truths* professional development method that anchors product managers with the skills most important for their professional success.

JJ is Chief Executive Officer of Great Product Management and has spent over 15 years as a product manager, product leader, and product management advisor, working with companies all over the world and across industries. She is faculty at Johns Hopkins University Whiting School of Engineering, teaching graduate level product management courses, and is also the host of the Product Voices podcast.

She has a Bachelor of Business Administration from Texas Tech University and a Master of Business Administration from Nova Southeastern University.

She lives in Dallas, Texas, and New York City with her wife and cats.

CONNECT WITH JJ

Twitter:	@jjrorie
LinkedIn:	LinkedIn.com/in/jjrorie
Instagram:	@jj.rorie
Email:	jjrorie@greatproductmanagement.com
Website:	GreatProductManagement.com

WHAT'S NEXT?

You can find all the information below on GreatProductManagement.com/bookstuff:

Additional Resources

I have created a collection of free online resources to help you in your journey of building the IMMUTABLE truths. These resources include templates and guides, suggested readings, people I like to follow, and more. You can find these resources at GreatProductManagement.com/freeresources.

Bring this Book into Your Organization or Classroom

If you would like your product team or students to read this book, you can buy it in bulk and receive a wholesale discount. Learn more at GreatProductManagement.com/bulk.

Corporate Coaching and Development

If you need a little extra guidance on implementing the IMMUTABLE truths, our coaching and training offerings may help. Learn more at GreatProductManagement.com/corporate.

Hire JJ To Speak

JJ Rorie is a dynamic, inspiring, and entertaining keynote speaker who can bring the IMMUTABLE truths to life at your next event or meeting. She can also speak on various other product management, business, and leadership topics. To learn more about how you can hire JJ to speak to your company or event audience, visit GreatProductManagement.com/speaking.

Podcast

JJ Rorie hosts the Product Voices podcast where she interviews diverse voices across the product management spectrum. The podcast is available on all major podcast platforms, or you can listen at ProductVoices.com.

CPSIA information can be obtained
at www.ICGtesting.com
Printed in the USA
LVHW070848070722
722948LV00004B/5

9 781955 985529